THE SEER'S JOURNEY

THE LIFE OF A VISIONARY PROPHET
& THE ULTIMATE ENCOUNTER

DONTRELL J. GREEN SR.

Copyright © 2023 Dontrell Green

All rights reserved, including the right to reproduce this book or portions thereof in any form whatsoever by author. No part of this book may be reproduced, scanned, or distributed in any print or electric form without author's prior expressed written consent. Please do not participate or encourage piracy of copyrighted materials in violation of author's rights.

To request permissions, contact the author at greendontrell41@yahoo.com

Scripture taken from the New King James Version®. Copyright © 1982 by Thomas Nelson. Used by permission. All rights reserved.

"Scripture quotations are from the ESV® Bible (The Holy Bible, English Standard Version®), Copyright © 2001 by Crossway, a publishing ministry of Good News Publishers. Used by permission. All rights reserved."

"Scripture quotations taken from the Amplified® Bible (AMPC),

Copyright © 1954, 1958, 1962, 1964, 1965, 1987 by The Lockman Foundation

Used by permission. www.lockman.org"

Scripture taken from the Holy Bible, NEW INTERNATIONAL VERSION®, NIV® Copyright © 1973, 1978, 1984, 2011 by Biblica, Inc.® Used by permission. All rights reserved worldwide.

Published By Writing in Faith
IAmWritingInFaith.com

Cover Design By Cherese Agee
Reseagee.com

Dontrell Green (Text)
ISBN 13: **979-8-9889051-0-3**

Dedication

I dedicate this book to my supernatural friends, the Angels of the Lord who are always encamped around me and who gave me this book in a dream three years ago. I also want to dedicate this book to my young twin prophets Dontrell Jr & Donzell who will one day be used greatly by the Lord to speak his Holy Word with precision and accuracy.

Acknowledgements

Writing this book was a huge challenge, but I wouldn't have gotten through it if it wasn't for my lovely wife, so without any further ado, I would like to honor and acknowledge my beautiful Queen, Lady Faith Green for standing beside me as I have taken out so much time and effort to write this amazing masterpiece of the Lord. Your countless prayers, love and support are beyond amazing, and I am forever grateful for it all. Thank you for holding me up, pushing me and always being the voice, I need the most when I want to give up. Everything you have done behind the scenes hasn't gone in vain, you're a blessing and a hidden jewel waiting to be revealed.

To my little ones, my bundles of joy and my legacy, I love you with an everlasting love just like our heavenly Father does. There is nothing I would not do for you, and you are the reason I smile. This book was specifically written for you as you begin to grow and mature. I want you to always know that there is something prophetic about your life and there is a holy call upon you that will lead you to a place of success and in leading an entire generation to Jesus. Always put God first in everything you do and live a life of purity, love, and faith. Daddy loves you and will never stop praying for you. Stay passionate, hungry, and zealous, for this is the key. Remember your father's voice and wisdom, A'lylah, Jace'yon, Dontrell Jr, Donzell, Devine, and Da'Zarea Green. Nevertheless, to the rest of you join the crew and know that my heart is big enough to love you also.

Remain humble, Promise, Adrianna and Brooklyn and God will see you through.

I also want to acknowledge my friends, my brother, Apostle Steven and my sister, Prophetess Crystal Halliburton. There is no way I could have finished this project without you. Over the years, your friendship has proven itself to be strong in me and my family's life and it is undeniably phenomenal. I have learned so much from both of you that I would have never known until we connected, from gleaning at your marriage, your diligence in the Word, your worship, and your hard work as you've received countless degrees and achievements. I love that you always keep it real, and your integrity is beyond words that can be explained. Thank you for all you do, and I look forward to continuing our covenant relationship together. We are the House of David and House of Johnathan in this modern-day era that many will learn what true covenant looks like.

Agents of Change & Transformation you never cease to amaze me in how many of you have grown and stuck with me during this last year of writing this book. I know I mentored many of you but there have been many days I have learned from you. Your eagerness to understand the prophetic makes me proud and causes me to rejoice knowing you will succeed as the Lord continues to raise you up and launch you forth. Thank you for your teachable heart and for deciding to allow me to mentor the best people on this side of heaven.

If there is a family I love to be around the most, it would be my Ignite Nations Global family. Thank you for giving me community and accepting me just the way I am. Many of you that are a part of this family have touched me in a special way and I will always cherish the moments we've shared as we come together to gather the nations on one accord for the name of Jesus. I pray as you read this book you will see a man you helped to shape and become a mouthpiece of God by your shield of protection and fence of love.

To my hometown, Lemannville, Louisiana, I will never forget where I came from and those who knew who I would become before I did. Thank you, Reverend Pastor, Joseph Coleman Sr., for showing me what a true preacher looks like and how we should always call on Jesus. Your walk with God has inspired me in such a profound way and I am forever thankful for your pour. The day when you decided to lay hands on me at the age of 8 years old has sparked a flame in me and today, I am a product of that anointing and will never lose sight of my heritage. Thank you, Buena Vista Baptist Church family, and the entire Lemannville community who always believed in me.

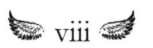

Author Endorsements

Dontrell Green is a prophetic voice that I admire and support. When I first met him, I could see the hand of God upon his life, so I had him join my broadcast "FROM THE MOUNTAINTOP" to pray and prophesy over many people. His accuracy and zeal were undeniable. I also love how he is an incredible father and husband. He has six children and loves them all very much. I endorse anything he puts his hand to do knowing that God will use him mightily. I am sure you will gain much insight from his book The Seers Journey.

Darren Canning
Darren Canning Ministries

In reading The Seer's Journey by Prophet Dontrell Green, you will see a clear visual of how a seer prophet is called, formed, and established by God through biblical scriptures and personal encounters. This book will help you to learn a new language from a seer prophet's perspective through dreams and visions and how to embrace the call and timing of the Lord while going through the process of the refiner's fire.

Tommy John Mota
Grace To Change

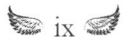

I have had the honor of knowing Prophet Dontrell and his lovely wife, Lady Faith, for a few years now. I have witnessed him ministering in person and was blessed to have him speak over my life, as well as over my husband's and children's lives. When Dontrell and Faith minister together, they flow as one, and their reciprocal display of honor, and unity, allows for an unhindered move of the Holy Spirit.

Prophet Dontrell is a modern-day prophet, who hears from God and sees in the spirit with precision and accuracy.

He carries his mantle with humility but with authority. He knows what he carries, he knows his position in the spirit, and he unapologetically speaks The Word of The Lord. As Dontrell ministers, you can feel the atmosphere shifting into another spiritual dimension. He ministers from a place of purity and speaks of heavenly revelations right from the heart of The Father.

As you journey through the pages of this book, you will find yourself relating to every story, and you will be filled with a desire to experience the supernatural in a whole new way!

Rosangela Atte
The Risings of The Esther's

Dontrell's newest book is a perfect resource for those seeking to increase the seer anointing upon their life. With an in-depth look at Dontrell's journey as a Seer Prophet, 'The Seer's Journey' taps into the realm a visionary prophet is required to steward and administrate within their prophetic mantle and mandate. The call of a Seer Prophet ushers the chosen vessel into experiences that are purely trusted through his relationship with the spiritual realm. As an emerging Prophet, Dontrell's dependency upon Holy Spirit is evident as he sees, foretells, and prophesies modern-day events in a timely and accurate manner. 'The Seer's Journey' gives the reader a glimpse of the personal pilgrimage Dontrell is traveling through by the power of the Holy Spirit. The grace upon Dontrell's life and the wisdom he releases throughout this book is one to glean from if you're hungry for a fresh impartation of insight into the mysteries and operations of Yahweh's Prophets. I am confident that those who yield their heart to the truth released through this ministry will, without a doubt, accomplish great exploits for the Kingdom of God during this crucial hour on the earth.

Holly Watson
Holly Watson Ministries
krgo.org

We are in a time when we need Seer prophets to arise like never before to see, perceive, and pay attention to what God is saying. The Seers of today must "see" what they say before they prophesy it because God is "watching" His word to perform it. In "The Seer's Journey" you will encounter the life of a Seer, the process the Seer goes through; the pitfalls, lessons, humility, and purity a Seer must walk in. Many of you will see yourself in the chapters of this lived out book. Let me tell you, Seers, you will all encounter the Lord in this book and many will be healed, delivered, restored, and positioned to walk in the mantle God has placed on your life from your mother's womb. I highly recommend you read this book.

Dontrell J. Green is a Seer/Prophet to Nations declaring, decreeing, prophesying, shamaring, and warning nations to turn back to the will and heart of God.

Wilmar Fernando Navarro
Founder, Mark of Love Ministry

The weight that has been placed on this prophetic voice, which is a gift to the Body of Christ, has been sealed by the hand of God. The Seer's Journey is a spiritual navigation that provides insight into the life of the Chosen. This book is filled with wisdom and knowledge to help you on the journey of becoming the best version of who God has called you to be. Prophet Dontrell's accuracy in the prophetic proves that one must live a consecrated life and walk closely with the Holy Spirit. The Lord has chartered his destiny to lead His people with a spirit of humility and love. An honest man with an authentic voice, a calling that has not been tainted, vision that is not obscured, and a posture of honor to the Almighty God. It is with great pleasure and honor to endorse a wealth of knowledge, The Seer's Journey.

Prophetess Kenita Milan
The R.O.C.K. Outreach

The Seers Journey is just that, a journey. This book will help Seers begin to navigate and understand their own process of preparation, as well as gain an understanding of their gifting. This book is full of revelation that I am sure for multitudes, will become as a training manual for the Seer.

Ruth Ann McCormick

Prophet Dontrell Green has done a masterful job in describing the process every Seer Prophet must walk through. The details of the pain that comes with the call and how God uses that to develop not just the gift but the character. This offers a sense of relief by giving the reader an understanding that what they are facing is not foreign to this office and if you're going through this, you're not off track but actually right where God needs you to be. As I read, I connected to the pain I too have had to process and the pitfalls I had to overcome because of the pain. Though this book is absolutely for now, I wish this book were available when I began my journey of development with God, as a Seer Prophet over 20 years ago.

Michelle M. Farrar

Author, Life Coach & Prophet

Prophet Dontrell is a man of God that brings purity and transparency. He shares his heart about how God has led him to where he is today. All the ups and downs of learning what the difference is between the Seer and the Prophet. He takes his gift seriously with scripture to back it up. This is only the beginning, Dontrell! Proud of you as this is your third book of many! Thank you for sharing your heart.

Bishop Diana E. Gill

Author of "You Call Me Beautiful"

Foreword

The prophetic can be a unique and sometimes difficult journey to embark upon. Many believers and prophets find themselves in places where they have unusual encounters and experiences that contain elements of mystery. When this occurs, it is vital that believers obtain understanding and revelation that will enable them to demystify their encounters. One of the purposes and goals of demystifying supernatural encounters is to give language to God-ordained experiences. In this sense, language serves as a tool that leads to clarity, revelation, and understanding regarding supernatural experiences. Since scripture is a composition of supernatural encounters, it is only appropriate for believers to consult the scriptures in hopes of understanding God's will for the supernatural.

One of the supernatural functions that God reveals in scripture is "The Seer." In ancient times, the seer was an individual that was graced with the gift of supernatural sight. From a biblical perspective, seers were individuals that were in divine communication, divine communion, and divine fellowship with God. It was from this place of communication, communion, and fellowship that God would give His seers the ability to see in a supernatural capacity. In ancient times, seers were also called prophets. Scriptural examples include 2 Samuel 24:11, 1 Chr. 21:9, Amos 7:12, to name a few. The seer played a vital role during that dispensation. The seer would often function as a consultant or advisor to kings. As such, God would relay messages to His seers through, dreams, visions, signs, symbols, ecstatic experiences(trance), and similitudes. The people of those days understood the importance of the seer. They understood the value of the seer. This understanding would compel them to render honor to the seer as God's oracle. In this present dispensation, it is important to clearly identify the role, function, value, and identity of the seer. This identification process starts with unveiling the "seer's journey."

To unveil the seer's journey, it is important to define the term journey. Webster's dictionary defines the term journey as follows: an act or instance of traveling from one place to another. This definition reveals the framework of the seer's journey. The seer's journey functions under the principles and governing oversight of prophetic processing. In this sense, prophetic processing works to enable the seer to transition from a place of immaturity to maturity in relation to their specific assignment as a seer. During this period of processing, the seer's calling is identified, they go through periods of discipleship, periods of supernatural experiences, periods of testing, periods of warfare, periods of isolation, periods of rejection, periods of instruction, periods of correction, and in some instances even periods of failure. This type of processing is designed to ensure that the seer is fully equipped for the work of the ministry. One of the ways that God initiates and accomplishes this process is by anointing men and women to create sound theological materials that function to help a person walk in their destiny and calling.

"The Seer's Journey: The Life of a Visionary Prophet and The Ultimate Encounter" by Prophet Dontrell Green, is a divinely inspired manuscript that functions to birth believers abroad into their purposes and callings as prophetic people. In the seer's journey, Prophet Dontrell Green provides a clear articulation of the principles of prophetic processing in the life of prophetic people. The Seer's Journey contains great revelatory insight regarding the divine agency that is commonly referred to as the prophetic. The Seer's Journey is not just an ordinary book. This book is filled with supernatural encounters, sound doctrine, and personal testimonies that if applied by the reader, will give a greater understanding of their calling and assignment. Now that you've purchased your copy of The Seer's Journey, I would like to encourage you to embark upon this prophetic adventure as Prophet Dontrell Green unveils "The Seers Journey: The Life of a Visionary Prophet and The Ultimate Encounter".

Prophet Steven C. Halliburton
The Brook Place Clarksville
Senior Leader

Table of Contents

Dedication iii

Acknowledgements v

Author Endorsements ix

Foreword... xv

Introduction... 1

Chapter 1: The Journey.. 5

Chapter 2: Purity... 15

    Purging To Cleansing 17

    Taking Responsibility 19

    Resisting Temptations 20

    Self Seeking Prophets 22

Chapter 3: The Encounter (I Shamar) 27

    I Shamar 34

        Examples 37

    Foresight...38

        Famine Is Coming:...39

        Nuclear Unrest & Bombings:..................................40

        New Train (Transportation) Inventions: 41

        Time Machines & Digital Currency:.......................42

        The Out Pour of The Spirit in Florida:..................44

        Blackouts and Radios 45

    Ending Notes 46

Chapter 4: Stewardship..47

    1. Prayer & Seeking...50

2. Writing & Journaling 54

 3. Studying The Word 57

 Encouragement 59

Chapter 5: Seers In Government **61**

 Remaining Uncompromised 63

 Carrying the Kingly Oil 66

 Final Thoughts 70

 Prophetic Utterance 70

 Leadership Wisdom 75

 Prayer of Activation 77

Book Recommendations **79**

Introduction

It all started back in the year 2017 when I noticed something was different about me. I would see things during the night through dreams and visions that I had never seen and had no explanation for. Though I always was a dreamer since my youth, however, I was now beginning to have more during this particular year, experiencing these awesome and tangible encounters that I had no articulation for. I remember wondering to myself if something was wrong with me and wondered if others were having these same experiences. I can recall when I would go back and forth to my pastor at that time, asking so many questions about what I was seeing and did not realize at the time that God was using all these moments to develop my skills as a young seer prophet. During that course of my life, I was modeling the example of Samuel the prophet without noticing it (read 1 Samuel 3:7) because of the level of honor and respect, I had for my spiritual father. He was indeed likening unto Eli during that season because of my immaturity to properly perceive the voice of God through the navigation system of sight. There would be times he would be able to help me and lead me in the right direction God wanted me to go, and then, there would be other times when he needed to pray more, or perhaps, he would push me to dig more inside of the Word of God and seek the Lord for myself. During this period of time, I discovered and learned about great men of God such as James Goll, John Paul Jackson, Bob Jones, Kim Clement, Brian Carn, etc. I found out over those two and half year's journey, that there was such a thing called a "seer". Although I had read many scriptures upon this and had heard this prophesied over many others during worship services and even myself, I was still buffed, clueless and ignorant of the terminology and its operations. I was led on a supernatural quest directed and guided by the Holy Spirit, learning and being trained those years for something that I would later be established in, teaching on and imparting. It is for this reason, I've longed and have been equipped; I write to help many of you who also desperately desire to understand this realm and who hope to see within the realms of the spirit with great precision, accuracy and clarity to combat the plans of the enemy and to see God's divine purpose manifest in and throughout your life. Well, what is a seer? All throughout the Bible, we can find that a seer was one who sees in the spirit with keen sight and who would gaze as well as peer through the unseen world and move within different dimensions. The word seer in the Bible is mentioned in the context of at least twenty-five passages of scripture and can be defined as one who sees with spiritual eyes, perceives and is another name for prophet. Nevertheless, the word itself occurs twenty-eight times in the King James Version of the Bible and is translated into two Hebrew words which are *chozeh* and *roeh*. A seer has revelatory knowledge and knowledge beyond his or herself but sees within the means of the eternal world by conveying it and interpreting it with the conscious mind. The seers are nothing short of visionary prophets who only respond and move by what they see and sense. The life of a seer-prophet lives for the encounter. They are beholders of glory in the unseen realm. Rather, it is for nations, people, personal visitations and pursuing to see Jesus, they live for the encounter because it is the very oxygen in which they breath. Not only do they see but they also operate profoundly with all five of their senses in the realms of the spirit. So much so, that Bob Jones calls them the entire Head according to Isaiah 29:10. Seers are God's supernatural change agents in the earth, and this is why in the days ahead, we shall begin to see an increase of seer prophets emerge. Those that will peer through the veil of heaven receive blueprints and scrolls. They will be trusted with secrets and mysteries from the throne room of God because they will be considered a friend of God. Did you know seers' dwell in the realms of dreams and visions? Yes, indeed all throughout Bible history, men were carried along by the spirit of God through the means of supernatural encounters. Seers walk a thin line between the heavens and the earth because their life is not their own. Angels accompany seers because they are divine messengers in the earth and govern the affairs of this world. Throughout this book, you will develop a passion to see and journey down a pathway that is unknown to man because supernaturally and extraordinary occurrences will suddenly take place. My heart desires that within the course of this book, I stir up and activate a hunger in you that cannot be quenched but that will propel you to want to see more and to help others around you. We are in an hour that the Lord is restoring the purity of the seer's anointing, and many will begin to seek out this grace that is lacking in the body of Christ and in the world at large. I strongly believe that many of the problems we are facing today in the world are because there is a scarce limit of true seers who are properly trained and who can see amid chaos. Another reason for writing this book is to restore the foundation of God's original purpose and plan for seer prophets and to help give language to an element of the prophetic that is not widely talked about in today's modern-day church. Many in this era of the body of Christ struggle within themselves with this gift and ability but can't often find words to express what they see because they are shattered by the opinions of men and, on many occasions, get rejected and don't have a place to help cultivate them or get the proper training they need. However, it is for this reason why God is raising up Samuels, who will teach the prophets and seers how to see with keen sight and teach them how to steward what they see. This group of Samuel prophets will be a group of individuals who have labored in the realms of the spirit and who understand what it means to see in hopes of bringing forth the next generation of seers and visionaries. One of the major key aspects and assets of a true seer is having wise fathers and mothers in their corner who can cheer them on as well as train and teach. I believe that as seers began to emerge and arise, we will see this merging of generations that will help advance the kingdom of God. I pray as you read this book, you will be empowered and that you, too, will be a part of that seer's company for a journey like no other.

(Formerly in Israel, if someone went to inquire of God, they would say, "Come, let us go to the seer," because the prophet of today used to be called a seer.)

Chapter 1

The Journey....

*The word of the Lord came to me, saying,
"Before I formed you in the womb I knew you, before you were
born, I set you apart; I appointed you as a prophet to the
nations."*

In this life, everyone has a start and a finish. As the saying goes, you must start somewhere, and you must crawl before you can walk. In the prophetic realm, it is the same concept, from budding to emerging and soon to becoming well-seasoned and mature within your sphere of influence and your prophetic mantle. We all have started somewhere, and all have had our share of ups and downs. Regardless of where you are, we all can agree it is a journey from start to finish. The call of a prophet is a huge honor and responsibility because it means you are valued in heaven, and it means you have been trusted by God to speak on His behalf for the world and all humanity. It is a special call and should never be taken lightly. As you step into your calling, you will realize everyone's calling from the Lord will be different and others supernaturally unique. It is through the journey we find expression of who we are and what God has called us to do. Through the wisdom of God, the journey was intended and created to equip you and was by no means created to limit you. One who is a mature seer appreciates this facet and understands it is the journey that marks them as a true visionary prophet and enables them to see even more. As a young seer, you must learn that patience helps to develop a greater sight as well as character for the assignment. Within the prophetic journey, there are some things you can only learn by going through the process of the journey. During this period, you learn the timing of God, the ways of God and the Father, to prepare you for the audience you are called to. If you get too impatient, you risk the opportunity of not carrying major keys that can only be given during the development stages. It is, for this reason, the journey teaches one how to walk patiently before the Lord, being anxious for nothing (read Philippians 4:6-7), but always trusting the Lord and remaining steadfast. In order to see effective success in the seer's ministry, he or she must learn the skill and patience of endurance. Every prophet will go through this period where they feel all hope is gone and God has forgotten about them, but true prophetic vision is birth behind the scenes when no one is looking. It is during these times that you are being tested and trained, where it is only you and the Holy Spirit. Have you heard the saying: "prophets are made in the cave"? Well, it is true; indeed, prophets are made in the cave and must pass through this journey of being consecrated, circumcised, and set apart by the Lord so that they may lead accordingly and in perfect alignment, fit for the master's use. For, in fact, it is the small things we learn along the journey that strengthen us for a promising future. Nevertheless, if it doesn't teach you anything else, it will teach you humility. Nowadays, it is too often in our current prophetic movements we find pride. I believe, like never before, in this hour, the Lord wants to take many back to the foundation of understanding the reason why they were called and take them on this journey to break up some of the pride and once more teach them humility so that there will be no mixture or selfishness within their hearts. There will be times God will take His prophets on a journey to show them what is in their heart and teach them humility. A prophet who does not submit to the correction and leading of the Lord is headed for destruction and will not properly lead others. Every prophet will have their own type of journey but must realize that each piece of that journey is necessary for where they are going and cannot be skipped by any means. Not only does the journey teach you humility and patience, but it places weight on your gift and releases a level of authority that allows you to have favor with man and with God. It is through the contacts and lenses of the journey; you gain strength and learn how to depend totally on God.

When I think about the journey, I think of something that is worth the wait and longevity. Something that will set you up for a lifetime and years to come, in order to establish you. Even Jesus himself had to go through a journey and great heroes such as, David, in order to rule well and to develop their kingship. During this phase, there is a transaction that takes place, and you build as well as have experience that will later bless you down the road. Nothing in life comes easy without first going through the process and I truly believe at this hour this is exactly what the Lord is doing with his seer prophets by bringing them into the refiner's fire. I can recall when I was first called into the prophetic ministry, how I had longed to hear and wanted to see visions and dreams. I thought that if I had all these encounters, it would prove that I was a prophet and that it would gain me some type of acceptance, but the danger in this is when we do this, we make it more about us than about God. I just knew if someone would have accepted my encounters or dreams, it would somehow take away the rejection I had smothered deep down inside, but to my knowledge I was wrong. That is why as a seer prophet the development stages and process are different from any other ministry because the Lord often must heal us from the trauma of rejection. Very often, a seer does not understand their value and has been purposely rejected by men, so it tends to cause them to shut down their gift and makes them never share again what they have been shown as well as causes their lenses to be tainted and their hearts to become bitter. I did not realize that at the beginning of my ministry, this was happening to me and somehow, the enemy had gotten a loophole into my life, and it was causing me not to see properly. However, this is another reason the journey is important because it helps you filter out the junk that's within your heart so that you may see clearly with purity and accuracy. There will be times God will allow rejection to come into our lives to show us what is really hidden within our hearts so that we may get the proper deliverance we need and so that we may learn humility and always give Him all the glory and not unto ourselves. Rejection is a major key in the developing stages of a true seer prophet. It is the cow manure and the fertilizer that helps grow you into the prophet you need to be. In ancient history, this was the same test Joseph had gone through before becoming second in charge over all of Egypt.

> Until the time came to fulfill his dreams, the
> LORD tested Joseph's character.
> **Psalms 105:19NLT**

In the life of Joseph, we can see that his steps were ordered by the Lord. Likewise, we are reminded that it is in the journey God is ordering our steps and guiding us into His perfect will and plans for our life. We should understand that His ways and plans are better and that if we trust Him, He will lead us to an expected end (read Jeremiah 29:11). Revelation during this time is birth and enhanced through the life of the seer prophet. It is through the means of the journey, revelation unfolds and given so that the seer can understand the divine will and intent of God. The journey offers no easy alternative, but it is directed to show one how to manage pain, how to deal with obstacles and it challenges you to arise above certain circumstances. However, the true journey starts within the mind and flows towards the heart before ever physically beginning. When there has been a pathway drawn out so great for a chosen vessel, it will first start in the mind and will require mental stability because the mind is the place revelation springs forth from and what vision is attached to. Therefore, this is the reason the enemy is always fighting the believer within the mind. The mind is a terrible thing to waste, to the extent that the scriptures urge us to keep our minds in perfect peace. If you are not careful, your mind will play tricks on you during the process of the journey, if you do not find peace or stay focused. It will make you think you are being punished instead of being refined or pruned for greatness.

> You will keep in perfect peace
> those whose minds are steadfast,
> because they trust in you.
> **Isaiah 26:3 NIV**

> "I the Lord search the heart and examine the mind,
> to reward each person according to their conduct, according to
> what their deeds deserve."
> **Jeremiah 17:10 NIV**

On many occasions, God will allow His seers-prophets to go through this process to keep them from entering the snares of the enemy or from making crucial mistakes that will result in prophetic pit falls. This teaches them discipline and allows them to value where they have started and reassures them that they are still human and not by any means exempt from the chastisement of God. Seers must embrace these facets so that they may be weighed and measured by God to receive new assignments and enter new realms of the spirit. A processed prophet is one who cannot be reckoned with and one who subdues the plans of the enemy when Satan plans to tempt or destroy them. When prophets truly allow God to process them, it helps them grow within their mantle and allows them to master gifts that were always locked within. What good is it to have a gift but not know how to properly use it? I believe the Lord is raising up seer prophets in this hour that will have a desire and spirit to want to learn and to be processed. There is an incubation period that takes place between the start and finish of a prophet that is by no means skipped so that they will be fortified to carry the blueprints from heaven for nations and regions. Nevertheless, when we fully surrender to the Holy Spirit during this period, we gain a greater respect for our office and never neglect to honor that which God has called us unto. The journey was made to refine you so that you would shine throughout the world like the diamond you are. Embrace the journey because as a seer-prophet, you have been called and stitched unto it.

As I ponder and think about the process diamonds go through, I am always reminded that God uses these same techniques to process us. When we are talking diamonds, we are talking about a jewel that is formed and made from the deep depth of the earth's surface. Most scientists that study diamonds have an understanding that they are forged through high pressure temperature and are very rare to find through the earth's crust.

Not only are they rare to find or come across, but in order to successfully retrieve diamonds, one must be willing to go into mines to get them. It is a fascinating process indeed and hard work is required but however, once this process is complete, diamonds are so incredible and brilliant among all humanity and are unmatched among any other material throughout the earth. Diamonds are valued at a high price and not just given to anybody but are precious at the elite level. Can I tell you that this is how God sees you prophet? You are precious and delicate to the almighty God, and this is why your process and journey are more strategic than others around you. No doubt, the fire in your life is being turned up and you are being stretched in more ways than usual, but it is all with the intent to make you the diamond you are. In addition, this is why you are not meant to fit in, the reason why many misjudge and misunderstand you. Your capacity to shine requires strategic instructions from beginning to end and if one instruction or ingredient is missing then you lose your flavor and signature of being the true prophet God has called you to be. You remain steadfast toward the process and understand you are the clay and the Father the potter.

Yet, O Lord, You are our Father;
We are the clay, and You our Potter,
And we all are the work of Your hand.
Isaiah 64:8AMP

With everything comes time and if we are not careful, we risk the chances of destroying vital and God-ordained moments that prove why we were called from the jump. You can either do two things; look at time as an enemy or embrace it as a friend that will soon loose you into your destiny. How you view the journey will be the key factor that will accelerate the time or keep you in holding bars. Listen, your perspective means everything along the journey. It was the children of Israel that can witness to this because they had a similar experience when they were relinquished out of the hands of Pharoah and left Egypt. A journey that was supposed to be 40 days turned into 40 years because their perspectives and mentality had not yet aligned with their move. It is possible that as we are in any process or transition, our feet are moving but our hearts and minds are still stuck in the past and it in turn limits our ability to grow and perceive. So, because of one's lack of perception, it blurs their vision, impacts their endurance, and stops their ability to trust what and where God is bringing them. The children of Israel's lack of trust in God put a major dent in their perception and caused them to stay in the wilderness longer than what was indented. Your response during the transition is very important and because they decided to complain rather than praise during their transition, God allowed them to wander for 40 years to get Egypt out of them. In fact, even Moses found himself carrying this same burden when God was only trying to cross His people over into the promise land. One of the most dangerous things that can happen is allowing other's' complaints to impact your judgment and cloud your decisions while amid a process or transition. Never allow the voice of another to be louder than the voice of God in your life unless you want to follow man rather than the path God has set before you. I learned a long time ago that if you follow God, you will never go wrong.

Yet, one of the most common things I have found about prophetic people is that many are upset with the journey when they should allow it to condition them. I believe a major part of why we have misplaced prophets in the body of Christ is because many have not stayed the course during the most important times and areas of the journey. With the children of Israel, we as a 21st century church can learn a lot about what not to do but use their struggles to capitalize and carve out a new generation of prophets and prophetic people who will have the tenacity and endurance to finish strong. After a season of much waiting and endurance, you must understand that you will eventually mount up on eagles' wings. There is a balance God is bringing his prophets through and it is a blend of the mountain-top experiences and valley-low crushing that you may be perfectly wired and equipped for kingdom service. Remember that if this never occurs, how can we then speak to people who are crushed and how will we have the language of those who have been at the mountaintop? The reality is we need both operations so that we may see the sunshine and the rain, and this is what the journey offers. Lastly, I encourage you that the journey gets a little bit better as you continue to yield unto the spirit of God and allow Him to have his perfect will, in and throughout your life. Remember you were built for the journey, and nothing works better than to walk the path that was set before you.

> But those who wait for the Lord [who expect, look for, and hope in Him] Will gain new strength *and* renew their power; They will lift up their wings [and rise up close to God] like eagles [rising toward the sun]; They will run and not become weary, They will walk and not grow tired.
> **Isaiah 40:31 AMP**

Dontrell Green

Chapter 2

Purity....

> Blessed *are* the pure in heart: for they shall see God.
> Matthew 5:8 KJV

In the prophetic ministry of the prophet and the lives of believers, it is no secret that purity must always be at the forefront. If nothing else matters, purity must always remain and be established in the life of God's prophets. Prophets must major in purity, there is no way around it. One of the most crucial things we are experiencing during this hour throughout the body of Christ and the current prophetic movement is impurity. It seems as if many have lost their reverence for holiness and have gotten caught up in a delusion of their gifts and supernatural experiences. There are many who operate from only a gift but lack the character of God. The church is in trouble because we have more microphones in the hands of many impure prophets and wonder why our churches are in chaos. If there has ever been a time purity needed to be restored in the body of Christ, the time is now. We are in a place where our faith depends on it. We need an emergence of pure prophetic voices to arise so that they can lead and guide the body of Christ back into repentance and the preparation for the second coming of Jesus Christ. Purity is not something we just do, but it is something we must live by in order to see God. Scripture is clear when it says only the pure will see God. Through this scripture, we see the importance of being pure in order to come before the king. Not only do we have to be pure in our actions, but the Bible says only the pure in "heart" will see God. True purity starts within the heart. You will always know what is truly in the heart of a man by the fruit that they bare. Seers, we must come to a greater understanding of what purity and holiness mean during this hour, yet we fall and stumble. I believe as we progress more in the prophetic there will be a deep cleansing that will take place. A cleansing that will not be denied, but that will produce and cause chains to be broken from the voices of those who desire to go deeper and higher in the things of God for such a time as this. Some of the key foundations the church has gotten away from are honor, honesty, and integrity. Somehow, we have grown to a place where many oppose the idea of honor and integrity and truly have no grit for honesty. We would rather put the focus on the popular as well as those who have a great following and influence. There has been great contamination that has swept in, and we are not able to recognize the real from the fake because societies aim to be liked and relevant. Yes, the church has done a disservice by making this distinction and refusing to break the narrative but has become the pitfall of a dying and impure generation that only speak with empty and carnal words. In order to break this delusion and cycle, seers must become the example once again and show the church and world at large what it means to carry the characteristics of God and what it means to remain pure, in regards to what is presented. However, this is why God must first bring his seer prophets through this process because they must become the plumb line in a world where it seems to be okay to be perverse. As we go further within this chapter, you will be taught how to sustain your purity and learn from some examples of what not to do as well as how you can be an example to others around you, as you gain a greater understanding of purity.

Purging To Cleansing

> "Woe to me!" I cried. "I am ruined! For I am a man of unclean lips, and I live among a people of unclean lips, and my eyes have seen the King, the Lord Almighty."
> **Isaiah 6:1 NIV**

Purging to cleansing is always required before we are ever promoted and elevated in the spirit, especially with prophets and those who desire to walk in such a calling. It is important as seer prophets we never neglect this operation but find ourselves daily killing our flesh through deep cleansing and purging upon the altar of God. Webster describes purge' as to: rid someone or something of an unwanted quality, condition or feeling. It is the force or removal and expelling of things that can no longer remain. Yet, when this takes place, there is a sudden change and transformation that takes place in the life of the individual, that not only occurs in their life, but also shifts the minds and hearts of those around them. Perhaps this is exactly what happens when God's prophets go through a process of deep cleansing and purging. They are separated from the world and from the familiarity of those who once knew them.

Throughout the Bible, we have witnessed many examples of great men who had to endure this journey in hopes to see their nation and people saved from the judgment of God and the oppression of its enemies. Take the Prophet Isaiah for example, he has an epiphany of God in the temple when King Uzziah dies. Within the description of this encounter, Isaiah describes this manifestation as a glorious moment that causes immediate repentance to take place on his behalf and causes his mouth to be cleansed and purged. Isaiah realizes that his life can no longer be the same and honestly repents concerning hanging around unclean people. This revelation and encounter with God changed his perspective which led to true deliverance and sudden transformation (read Isaiah 6:6-7). Atmospheres indeed create safe environments for repentance and encounters for the spirit of God to dwell. In this example of Isaiah, we can learn and gain an understanding that we must be a separated people but most importantly, prophets with clean lips. Even Jeremiah had to accept and learn this concept when the Lord reached out to touch his mouth (read Jeremiah 1:9). Both prophets had to undergo surgery in order to be used by God. Their mouths had to be filtered out to get rid of excuses, gossip, and the speech of man that they may be fully equipped to be the spokesman of the Lord. After undergoing this process, they both succeed in being two major prophets in the Bible, whose words did not fall to the ground and who both prophesied the coming of Jesus Christ in their day and time. In addition, this is why I encourage prophets to get purged. It is also wise to stay away from gossip and slander and those who seek to speak evil of others, yet you become polluted and tainted. These are serious tactics and pitfalls one must be aware of if you hope to sustain your purity and reputation as a seer prophet. Purging and cleansing must become a priority and second nature to the life of the prophet and he or she cannot risk otherwise less the entire body crumbles. You purge not for your own purpose but for the purposes of others around you, so that others will not be affected by the things which have infected you. Prophets must learn that it is okay to detox at certain periods of your life, so that God may pour back into you. Where there is a purging there is an emerging.

Purge me with hyssop, and I shall be clean: wash me, and I shall be whiter than snow.
Psalm 51:7 KJV

TAKING RESPONSIBILITY

> David said to Nathan, "I have sinned against the Lord." And Nathan said to David, "The Lord also has allowed your sin to pass [without further punishment];
> you shall not die.

A true sign of one's maturity and purity is when one can take responsibility for their own actions rather good or bad. Being able to take responsibility shows the true definition of your character and your morals as well as values. There is no better alternative than to take responsibility when you have done something wrong rather than to run, hide or give no response at all. In the life of David, we can find a man who was caught in sin at the time of his adulterousness with Bathsheba and is confronted by the prophet Nathan. He gave no excuse or restraint but took his correction like a mature adult. Therefore, even within the contents of this story, we learn a very important lesson and principle of the prophet's ministry, and that's to always be ready to confront wickedness and sin, no matter what (at any given cost or at whatever level) be ready to confront the thing which grieves the heart of God. Nevertheless, David was not afraid to admit and take responsibility for his actions by confessing to the prophet he was wrong and had sinned. His transparency and honesty opened the door for the mercy of God and caused God to spare his life. It is too often I run into people during this day and time who are too prideful in admitting when they are wrong and who would rather hide their sinful ways than come forth with repentance and confront their transgression. David understood what he had done was wrong and knew the only way to get back into the right standings with God was by taking responsibility. If we are going to see true authentic prophetic ministry in this current hour, we must raise up men and women who are willing to take ownership of their actions no matter the outcome, who will learn from their mistakes to become better people and vessels for the masters' uses. If we do not do this, we risk the chances of raising a bunch of liars and deceitful people who would rather hoard their sins and never allow God to forgive them so that they may grow in wisdom from their errors. There is freedom when we take responsibility, for our actions and guilt no longer can keep us bonded. Your taking responsibility will always be predicated on how deep and desperate you're willing to become pure before the father.

If we confess our sins, he is faithful and just and will forgive us our sins and purify us from all unrighteousness.
1 John 1:9 NIV

RESISTING TEMPTATIONS

Submit yourselves, then, to God. Resist the devil, and he will flee from you.
James 4:7 NIV

Your greatest challenge in the prophetic journey will always be getting over the hurdle of temptations. The devil, your adversary is always looking and seeking a way to deceive and entice the believers. Rather it is through sexual perversion, greed, or material things you will always be tempted to give into things which separate you from the will and presence of God. Satan uses no new tricks but uses your own fleshly desires against you in hopes to pull you away from the purposes of God and to find fault in you, that he may use it to accuse you before the throne of God (read Revelation 12:10). It is, for this reason, we need to renew our minds daily and empty our hearts of selfish ambitions regularly that we may not become prone unto his devices. We must follow the example of Christ on an everyday basis that we may use the Word of God to fight off his tactics. When you walk honestly and purely before God, there will always be something that will try to come to taint and corrupt what you stand for. In your response, you must not give into temptation, but it is a divine moment to seek the presence of God more, that He may give you peace, wisdom, and strength. It was, for this reason, Jesus won the battle against the devil in the wilderness when He allowed the spirit of God to fight on his behalf and summited to the Word of God (read Luke 4). During your darkest hour of temptation, it is important as believers we have a Word within our spirit that we may not sin against God.

> I have hidden your word in my heart
> that I might not sin against you.
> **PSALM 119:11 NIV**

No matter how big or great the temptation may be, never think Heaven is not watching to see how you react or respond to the occasion. All throughout the Bible, we find great men and women who have been tempted at the most important hour to see if they would hold or fold. Some overcame that temptation and others failed, but nevertheless, it is always the challenge of every born-again believer to endure this process. In addition, when you can overcome temptation, you gain authority over it, and it is no longer a stumbling block in your life. You will triumph over it, and it will help others gain victory over it as well.

Gehazi is a perfect example of a person throughout biblical history who did not overcome temptation but gave into it because of his unwillingness to obey and relinquish his selfish greed (read 2 Kings 5:19-

27). Not only did he disobey his leader by taking gifts from Naaman, but he also lied and tricked Naaman into giving him all the money that Elisha had refused. Gehazi's greed led him into a place of dishonesty, and he was willing to do whatever he needed to do so that he may achieve what he desired. However, this is why it is so imperative we do not give in to temptations because it leads to a dangerous place of deceit, greed, and brokenness. The moral of the story is because of Gehazi's poor decision to follow the instruction of his leader he was cursed with a curse and had to endure leprosy the rest of his life. When we give in to temptation, it opens the door to sin, which will later lead us to the pathway of death and spiritual blindness. Decide today to resist every form of temptation and live at peace with the plan God has for your life.

No temptation has overtaken you except such as is common to man; but God *is* faithful, who will not allow you to be tempted beyond what you are able, but with the temptation will also make the way of escape, that
you may be able to [a]bear *it.*
1 Corinthians 10:13 NKJV

SELF SEEKING PROPHETS

Hear this, I am against the prophets," says the Lord, "who use their [own deceitful] tongues and say, 'Thus says *the Lord.*'
[32] Hear this, I am against those who have prophesied false *and* made-up dreams," says the Lord, "and have told them and have made My people err *and* go astray by their lies and by their reckless boasting; yet I did not send them or command them nor do they benefit *and* enhance [the life of] these people in the slightest way," says the Lord.
Jeremiah 23:31-32 AMP

In every generation and especially the time we are living in now, there always seem to be false and self-seeking prophets to arise among the believers. These prophets have no intent on bringing glory unto God but rather unto themselves. Self-seeking prophets are those who only want the spotlight on them and who speak with flattery tongues and who do not have the true Word of the Lord in their mouths, which leads to lies and manipulation. They speak with empty imaginations and the Spirit of God is nowhere prevalent among them. Yet, they are false proclaiming to be true and stealing the Words of God's true ordained prophets. It is obvious we are living among them today and somehow the church has harbored a pattern of accepting these types of prophets rather than exposing and expelling them from our mist. The reality is they are self-seeking prophets and are ruining our ability and capacity to truly hear the heart of the Father. When self-seeking prophets are among the camps of the believers, they only tell you what you want to hear and disregard the true message of the Lord. They carry popular and gullible words but not words that are beneficial, weighty, or sustainable. Self-seeking prophets only live for the moment and never the future. As you dive deeper into your place of purity, you must be aware of these types of prophets and know the spirit they operate from. Perhaps, they only operate off your emotions and are more dangerous than psychics leading God's people astray and from his word as well as his presence (read Deuteronomy 18:20). Indeed, this is why the Bible says to believe not every spirit and that we have a surer word of prophecy through the Word of God. When false prophets come, they only come with the intent to rob God's people (fleecing the flock of the pasture) and are more prideful and arrogant than ever. Yes, they are wolves in sheep's clothing, soon to harm and hurt the body of Christ with their impure and dirty claws.

If the church plans to survive the tough times ahead, she must be willing to expunge these prophets who carry heresy and contempt. One who was known for this type of behavior in the Bible was the wicked and false prophet Balaam. In the book of Numbers of the Bible, it is proven that Balaam carried a lot of these same characteristics and later betrayed Israel and led them astray (read Numbers 22,23,24,25). He was hired by the enemies of Israel and was assigned to curse them. Balaam's heart was far away from God and not right. Not only was his heart not right with God, but he also offered up false sacrifices to try to curse and destroy the children of Israel. Balaam carried a tongue of enticement and eventually caused Israel to stumble through the means of perversion with prostitutes and idolatry all to be given a reward from King Balak. False prophets like Balaam will do anything to please themselves, even if that means selling their souls for financial gain, they will stop at nothing to get it because they are self-seeking.

But I have a few things against you, because you have there some [among you] who are holding to the [corrupt] teaching of Balaam, who taught [a]Balak to put a stumbling block before the sons of Israel, [enticing them] to eat things that had been sacrificed to idols and to commit [acts of sexual] [b]immorality.
Revelation 2:14 AMP

In essence, to the close of this chapter, I would like to remind you of your duty and integrity to remain pure as you soar higher in your prophetic ministry so that you may sustain true intimacy and holiness before the father. The more purity you possess the more God establishes you. Don't be known for your gifts alone but be known as one who carries the traits and the fruit of the spirit by keeping your character intact and by always remaining pure. Your ascension will always be based upon your level of purity.

> Who may ascend onto the [a]mountain of the Lord?
> And who may stand in His holy place?
> He who has clean hands and a pure heart,
> Who has not lifted up his soul to what is false,
> Nor has sworn [oaths] deceitfully.
> **PSALM 24:3-4 AMP**

Chapter 3

The Encounter (I Shamar)

After this I looked, and behold, [a]a door standing open in heaven! And the first voice which I had heard, like the sound of a [war] trumpet speaking with me, said, "Come up here, and I will show you what must take place after these things."
REVELATION 4:1 AMP

It all began back in the year 2006, as far as I can remember, a time when the Lord first encountered me at a pizzeria which caused me to become curious and seek after Him more. I was encountered by an angel of the Lord that was in human form. This angel told me things about myself I had no idea of, but that I knew was true. It was at this moment in my life, I knew God was real and there was something different about my life. During that same year, I started to have more dreams and visions throughout the night and became overly interested in what I would see and hear. However, at that time I had no language or terminology concerning what I was being shown. I was a seer all the long but did not have the proper people or resources to help equip me or cultivate me. It was not long before my seer sight began to slowly diminish. One of the things seers must understand is your environment matters. Though we can have encounters anywhere or at any time because we can never limit God, it is still important we find ourselves in the right environments and among the right people so that our gift may continue to be sharpened, and that our gauge is focused. Since my ability to see began to become blurry and I was not having encounters like I used to, it took years before I started having encounters again because I became a product of my environment. I was young and immature and did not understand what was going on in my life. So, a gift that was made just for me was placed on a shelf until I could properly use and understand it. From 2006 until the year 2014, there was a cap on my gift. Yes, a cap or a veil rather that was there until I met my pastor who during the time had just started a new church. I knew from this point I had the chance to regain my sight because this was a church that understood the gifts of the spirit and didn't think the encounters I had in previous years were crazy or weird but embraced the gifting of God in my life. I soon became intimate once more with the presence of God and it was not long before I again started to have dreams and visions like I did back in 2006. The whole concept was, I needed a place where I could be me. A place where I could encounter God, be free and unashamed. Most seers never fully develop because they do not have a safe haven or leaders that will pour into them, leading and directing them to where they should go or what they should do. By this time in my life, I was enjoying the moment and learning all I could but still would ponder on the encounter I had at that pizzeria. That encounter stuck with me, and I found myself yet again searching for more and trying to make sense of it. The time was passing, I had done some great things outside of the church for God and was serving my pastor faithfully. We both knew I had a call on my life, I just had not figured out how I would embrace it and honestly, I didn't think I was worthy to even preach God's Word. I was scared and nervous because I did not think I knew enough and felt uneducated, but there were always these voices that said 'he doesn't call the qualified, he qualifies the called'. That saying truly resonated with my spirit and I continued to follow the voice of God and serve my pastor. In 2015, my life was upside down,

I mean everything that could go wrong was going wrong, I was still unsure if I wanted to do ministry, I had somewhat of a worldly mindset and definitely wasn't living according to the Bible. My entire life had taken a spin and I desperately needed God but felt so out of touch with Him because I felt the spirit of condemnation and guilt eating me up. My mom had died that same year and my dad got into a terrible car accident that left me in tears and wondering where God was. I remember weeks after both events had happened. I was over at my dad's house sitting in the living room at the time with him and my stepmom when suddenly, we heard a knock at the door. A unfamiliar man was at the door saying he was my dad's therapist nurse and had come to help him get back on his feet due to the recent accident. Well, little did I know this was the angel of the Lord yet again in human form sent there to instruct me and allow my dad to be an eyewitness of what was on my life. I was sitting on the sofa opposite of my dad when this man pulled up a chair close to my dad to talk with him. Not knowing what was being communicated, I continued to play on my cell phone when I heard the man say loudly "if you make it through this, you'll see your son have one of the biggest churches in this city". I immediately took off running in the house because I knew this was the Lord speaking to me about my calling yet again. Eventually, the man took off to leave right after saying this, but my parents did not have his number and there was no information left, so my dad tried to catch him at the door, but he had literally disappeared in the wind. Later, my stepmom tried calling my dad's doctors and health care providers to get his information and see when the next appointment would be, but they found out that the providers had never sent any one out. I knew then this was the angel of the Lord sent to give me a message. I had another encounter after all those years but during a trying time in my life, where I wanted to give up and I thought it was all over. God sent his angel to comfort me and assure me of my calling. This type of encounter is likened to the same one Jesus and Hagar had after and during a tough situation.

> But the Angel of the Lord found her by a spring of water in the wilderness, on the road to [Egypt by way of] Shur And He said, "Hagar, Sarai's maid, where did you come from and where are you going?" And she said, "I am running away from my mistress Sarai." The Angel of the Lord said to her, "Go back to your mistress, and submit humbly to her authority." Then the Angel of the Lord said to her, "I will greatly multiply your descendants so that they will be too many to count." The Angel of the Lord continued.
> **GENESIS 16:7-10 AMP**

> Then the devil leaveth him, and, behold, angels came and ministered unto him.
> **MATTHEW 4:11 KJV**

The reality is that God will always be with us even through our most difficult situations. He will send his angels as messengers to comfort and assure us of what He has called for us to do. One of the major aspects of a seer is they will have a strong angelic presence that will accompany them. At the time, I did not realize it, but the Lord was allowing me to see and witness the angelic assistance that accompanied me. As a seer, you will go through different periods of your life where the Lord will open your eyes to see within the unseen realm to see exactly who and what is accompanying you (read 2 kings 6:17). Never take this lightly but embrace it and honor these supernatural experiences. What you encounter is eternal and should never by any means necessary be mocked or mishandled. This is why in the days ahead, I believe God will raise up experienced and mature seers who are sensitive unto his spirit that He may reveal some hidden things unto them that will hit the face of the earth. We are coming into the days when what was concealed will be revealed. There will be a greater accuracy that will fall upon the prophets and a greater precision to fall on the seers that the plans of God will be manifested and demonstrated throughout the world. Seers are a different breed, and not only do they encounter the awes of God, but they see with a distinctive sight that helps shape and guard nations against impending dangers. In the seers well, are warnings and directives for nations as they convey the heart, mind and will of God. Did you know that seers are more prone to tread through uncharted territory? Yes, indeed the life of a seer must be willing to move with obedience, resilience, and boldness. Their life is truly a faith walk believing and trusting upon the Holy Spirit to carry them and lead them into the unknown. A seer is a risk-taker and God expects nothing more than radical obedience from his seers. The heart of the seer is in the hand of God. Seers will always reveal the heart of the Father and see how he sees a matter. This is why it is important as seers, to keep our hearts and motives pure. Mature seers understand they cannot afford to miss by only looking at the exterior but must see the interior of a person's heart and the core of the situation. Take Samuel for example, he was instructed to anoint a new king for Israel and had to select a son of Jessie but was about to miss it because he was looking at the exterior rather than the heart of the person (read 1 Samuel 16:7). God in that moment taught the prophet a valuable lesson. We should never judge a book by its cover but should always seek the Father no matter what and see how he sees. Sometimes, as seers, if we are not careful, we can get so comfortable and content in our gift that we can neglect seeking God. When we allow this to happen, we miss God and can cause a people or an entire nation to go astray as well as walk in error. We should never get so caught up in our gift that we forget our seek and fail to consult God. One of the most dangerous things I see in the current prophetic movement is, we have vessels who have forgotten their scck. Yes, they have lost their ability in seeking the Holy Spirit for words concerning their nation and people and have made decisions based on logic and reason because they rather depend merely on their gift and not the leading of the spirit. True seers-prophets understand their gift means nothing if it is not being driven by the Holy Spirit. I prophetically decree this is the hour and season prophets and prophetic voices are finding their seek once again. A time we will find greater intimacy with the Father and peer beyond the veil seeing the way Heaven sees and knowing exactly how we should conduct ourselves for the seasons ahead. I declare the Father will make us meek for the seek and nothing should stand in our way that will get us off course in the mighty name of Jesus Christ.

> Blessed and favored by God are those who keep His testimonies, And who [consistently] seek Him and long for Him with all their heart.
> **PSALMS 119:2 AMP**

However, it is the seek that opens the realms of encounter. I remember back in 2019 while at work doing some maintenance work, I started having a strong desire for the presence of God, there was a hunger and a thirst. I would always worship and found myself many times weeping and praying believing to encounter God in a fresh way. I recall going all day from the start of work until I got home seeking God because I was desperate to encounter him. One night, I remember waking up in the middle of the night and hearing the Spirit of God say, AA Allen in my ear but did not understand what was being conveyed. I just simply went back to sleep knowing I had to be up early in the morning. Well, the next morning while preparing for work, those words were in my heart all day. I found myself studying and watching YouTube videos of AA Allen's legacy and what he had accomplished in the gospel. I then began to read this new book I had just gotten from Apostle Ryan Lestrange called "Higher Dimension" during my lunchtime but did not get the chance to finish reading it because, of course, I was at work. Once lunch was over, I found myself back watching YouTube. I ran across a video of Sid Roth "It's supernatural" and was listening to a well-known prophet at the time mentioning the next wave and move of God that was coming. I found myself once again becoming hungry and desperate for God. By this time, I was soon to get off from work but on my way home, my wife had to stop by the store to pick something up. I decided to stay in the car and finish reading my book 'Higher Dimension'. I can record reading a chapter on the apostle being unlockers and came across a sentence that mentioned the late Prophet Rev. Kenneth Hagin. Within a split second, my eyes began to be blurry and everything around me seemed as if it was moving. I was caught up in a trance state moment and a daze, where I was suspended between the natural realm and the unseen realm. It was then I felt a huge hand within my belly that moved very largely from side to side then I was back to consciousness. Immediately, I burst out into speaking in tongues and the spirit of joy and laughter hit me uncontrollably. My wife asked why I was laughing once she got back in the car, but I could not explain, all I knew was I was having an encounter. From that one encounter, it built my faith to seek God more and trust His timing. That night before, I would have never known I would have an encounter if I would not have taken out time to seek God. In my response to seek him more concerning what He was saying to me, opened the door to an unusual encounter that I will always remember. When we press in for the glory of God, the impossible happens and we receive a touch from Heaven. Nevertheless, the same encounter and experience AA Allen and Prophet Kenneth Hagin had encountered, I also encountered. I received the same impartation from just studying and reading about them. Since then, I've had numerous encounters because I never allowed my seek to die but stayed meek within my seek. When we take out time to seek the Father, it shows how hungry we are for His presence but most importantly, our humility. Humbling ourselves is not a sign of weakness but a sign of submission and honor. Those who are humble will encounter God. Sometimes there are blinders on our eyes because of the pride within our hearts and from not truly humbling ourselves. Sometimes blinders are only there because it is predicated on our seek and sometimes blinders are there because we've gotten too familiar with what was and the God of the encounter. It is important in this hour as seers we remain teachable and open so that the Spirit of God can have free course in our lives so that we may go to higher heights and deeper depths. The encounter was made to take you deeper and to realms you have never known.

I SHAMAR

> "Son of man, I have appointed you as a watchman to the house of Israel; whenever you hear a word from My mouth, warn them from Me.
> **Ezekiel 3:17 Amp**

In the prophetic journey, the symbol of the eagle represents the prophet because of its ability to see with keen sight and its ability to soar upward towards the sun. Did you know eagles can see at long-range distances? Studies show that eagles can see small details from a long distance away with estimates suggesting that they can see up to 2 miles away when flying at an altitude of 1000ft. This skill set allows them to locate and capture prey with extreme precision no matter the distance or range. Their incredible sight gives them an advantage over an average human whose visual acuity index is 20/20. Eagles are amazing creatures and spiritually speaking, the seer-prophet is compared to the eagle. This is why God has placed seers as watchmen to watch in the distance, to protect, to warn and to Shamar (to guard). One of the strong abilities of the seer will always be their sight, in fact, their eyes are a weapon of warfare. What the seer sees can stop the plans of the enemy and can save an entire nation and people. The seer hears God with their eyes. In other words, they communicate with God through the lenses of their eyes. They can see something and know exactly what is being communicated. It's just like sign language; they see words, numbers, shapes, sizes, etc. but know without a doubt what is being conveyed to them from Heaven's perspective. God has gifted them and charged them to be supernatural agents on earth. They are the policemen or CIA perhaps who watch in the unseen realm, spying, patrolling, and severing the body of Christ with their warnings and foresight of the future. Before anything happens on the earth, seer-prophets will be notified.

Surely the Lord God does nothing Without revealing His secret plan [of the judgment to come] To His servants the prophets.
Amos 3:7AMP

I like to call and define seers as the alarm systems that go off in the earth during crisis or any major catastrophes. When seers sound the alarm, the body of Christ must take the time to pay attention and take heed to what is being addressed. It's no secret that they are multifaceted because not only do seers have the ability to see profoundly but they have access to all five senses which means they are keen at hearing, feeling, tasting, seeing and smelling. Seers are unique and because of this grace, it is hard to deceive them without attacking their core abilities. For this reason, this is why the spirit of Jezebel is always coming up against them and they are always receiving persecution from their critics. All of this is to discourage the seer and cause them to relinquish their authority. When the seers leave their post of watching, the enemy knows he has the leverage because he can now come in on the church unaware because the seer is emotionally distracted and there has been no clear sound of the enemy's arrival. They Shamar (guide) the church and even the world at large to a place of safety and position them for the coming storm. When seers are in their rightful place, there is nothing that can stop the momentum and process of the church. I believe over the past few years the church has done a horrible job by not accepting and receiving these Shamar prophets. I believe because of their lack of understanding they have only recognized them as doom and gloom prophets when they were sent as gifts to protect and mobilize the church. Shamar prophets carry the future whether for good or bad, they will know the times and seasons just as the son of Issachar did when Israel found themselves wondering what they should do and how they should prepare (read 1 Chronicles 12:32). As a young Shamar prophet myself, I've found myself often getting downloads from Heaven concerning my nation and various nations as well as impending judgments that are to come. It is important to understand that as a Shamar prophet, you will receive foresight based on the jurisdiction you've been authorized to watch over. The process of being the watchman for that region or territory means receiving intel and being able to intercede on behalf of its government and people. Having the courage and boldness to stand in the gap and dismantling any plans or tactics coming against its fortress. "I Shamar" does not just mean having great sight or being accurate but it means standing in the gap, covering and being on the frontlines, the first on duty for war. Shamar prophets' duty is to war in the spirit until the situation is resolved in the spirit and it holds no sign as a threat.

> I will stand at my guard post
> And station myself on the tower;
> And I will keep watch to see what He will say to me,
> And what answer I will give [as His spokesman] when I am reproved.
> ² Then the Lord answered me and said,
> "Write the vision and engrave it plainly on [clay] tablets
> So that the one who reads it will run.
> ³ "For the vision is yet for the appointed [future] time
> It hurries toward the goal [of fulfillment]; it will not fail.
> Even though it delays, wait [patiently] for it,
> Because it will certainly come; it will not delay.
> **Habakkuk 2:1-3 AMP**

Another key element of the Shamar prophet is, we do not just pray or see but we document what is being shown. All throughout scripture, we find prophets who had this type of grace who documented that which they would see. When things are not written, it is hard for the audience you are called to, to believe what is coming out of your mouth is true. It is also a reflection and irresponsibility of your character to trust you with any secrets or plans God has for the world. When you do not write things down, you are illegally operating in the spirit and what you say holds no value or authority.

Examples:

> In the [a]first year of Belshazzar king of Babylon Daniel had a dream and visions appeared in his mind *as he lay* on his bed; then he wrote the dream down and related a summary of it.
> **Daniel 7:1AMP**

> So write the things [a]which you have seen [in the vision], and the things [b]which are [now happening], and the things [c]which will take place after these things. **REVELATION 1:19AMP**

> The word which came to Jeremiah from the Lord: ² "Thus says the Lord God of Israel, 'Write in a book all the words which I have spoken to you.
> **Jeremiah 30:1-2AMP**

FORESIGHT

I used to think I was crazy and thought no one would ever believe me because of the visions and dreams I was receiving over the years until God made it clear to me and through various people that I was a watchman, a Shamar prophet. Did you know that the future is not promising until a prophet is born? In the DNA of a prophet, we carry the future, and the future cannot come until we announce it. When prophets speak, realities are created and the Heavens are open, things come into existence and the future is formed. Therefore, this is why prophets should never get upset when being rejected because once you understand your value, you understand it is not really you that is missing out, but those who reject you. One of the hardest things a seer-prophet will have to endure is being ignored knowing you have received a warning or instruction from the Lord, but the people reject that word or do not take heed. However, they did not reject you but rejected God by their ignorance and rebellion (read

Luke 10:16). Continue to stand firm on what the Lord said unto you and watch as it surely shall come to pass.

> Call to Me and I will answer you, and tell you [and even show you] great and mighty things, [things which have been confined and hidden], which you do not know and understand and cannot distinguish.'
> **Jeremiah 33:3 AMP**

Famine Is Coming:

During the summer months of July 2018, on the fourth day, I was given a dream that night of what was to come into America and the nations abroad. In the dream, I found myself within a grocery store and I saw what looked like a security system set up all throughout the store, that was there to limit and control the number of people who could come in as well as the amount of food that can go out. All throughout the aisles of the store shelves were empty and had a limited supply of food and products. Within the dream, I saw people scrambling, some were stealing food and others were making price changes because many could not afford the food. As they would leave the store, many were required to show a form of ID in order to get out of the store and then the dream was over. Upon waking from this dream, the Holy Spirit spoke and said a famine would come to the Land of America and it would cause great turmoil and distress among its people and economy. The security system was set in place to sustain a limited number of people and control the narrative of what was being distributed in hopes of surviving and living. The Lord spoke and said this will catch many by surprise and this will cause much chaos and even violence within stores, homes, and neighborhoods. I then heard the Lord say, tell my people to prepare, prepare for the storm that is ahead and brace yourselves for more surveillance watches in your cities as well as identification profiling and searches. Famine will come and catch many off guard. It is time to rise from your slumber America and take heed as I have given you chance after chance says the spirit of the Lord. After this download, I was stunned with shock and the fear of the Lord. I knew our only chance of survival was to begin stocking up and preparing for the coming storm. From this dream encounter and foresight five years earlier, I still can hear the Father saying, "prepare, for the time is now".

Nuclear Unrest & Bombings:

On March 7, 2019, I was given a weird and horrifying dream concerning bomb threats coming to the state of Pennsylvania. While in this dream, I remember watching these two little kids get in a taxicab with a strange-looking foreign guy. There was another guy who appeared to be American, screaming from across the street "STOP THEM". No one in the city among the crowds paid any attention. The two kids and this stranger continued to approach getting in the car and the man who was screaming continued to scream. The stranger proceeded to get out of the car to fix his suitcase and I was able to see the kids also as they stepped out of the car. When the kids reached down to tie their shoes, their coats opened, and I saw what looked like suicide bomb vests. They eventually got back in the car and drove off. I was then suddenly awakened and began to ponder on what I was shown. I heard the spirit of the Lord say, bomb threats and havoc in the state of Pennsylvania. To my common mind, I still did not understand what this meant and what I was supposed to do concerning what I was shown, being that I was not from this particular state. I was given another dream on April 6, 2019 (God speaks once yet twice; read Job 33:14). That night, I recall going to sleep early because I had to go to work the next morning. I found myself falling asleep and going into a dream where I was with a prominent prophet in a meeting room or prestige conference space. As we were in this room, I remember sitting at a table across from him and he spoke to me saying there was going to be an explosion in the state of Pennsylvania. He said there would be a fight over nuclear unrest throughout the nation and superior power over these weapons. I was then informed by the prominent prophet within the dream that there would be talks of new nuclear weapons that we have not yet seen or heard of. The dream ended, and I awoke from this dream aware of exactly what the Lord was showing me. I heard the Lord say, pay attention and pray against suicide bombers and pray for our youth. At that moment I pressed into prayer. The Lord said, wicked and corrupt deals will be made from the courts of Pennsylvania and there will be explosions and bomb attempts that will come from the hands of evil men. The Lord said, there shall be more terrorist attacks and domestic violence, but I have equipped you today and it will not stand if my people who are called by my name would humble themselves and pray. Nations will continue to target you America until they know exactly what is in your arsenal. For this reason, I have fortified you and will keep you, says the Lord. Let it be known there shall be nuclear unrest and bomb threats, but I am sovereign and have not changed my mind concerning you.

New Train (Transportation) Inventions:

Get ready for innovation concerning the railroad industries, technology, and new inventions of trains. 4 years ago, I was given a dream where I was taken to the future by the angel of the Lord. I remember it like it was yesterday. It was during my birth month of April, I remember being in this dream talking to a teacher from my past, then leaving him and getting in a car with my high school coach (who represented the angel of the Lord). As I got in this car with him, he began driving and I was seated on the passenger side. We approached this "train track" and the car we were in was black, but it had no tires. The train track was up high in the air and about the same height as a skyscraper building, which had rails around the top made of brick with electrical girds surrounding it. As we drove upon the train tracks; in front of us were TWO TRAINS that looked brand new, something I have never seen in our modern day and time. It looked like something out of the future. When I woke up the next morning, I sought the Lord on the matter, and He said we will see a new invention concerning the model and make of trains. I never spoke about the dream publicly but kept the dream in mind. I was shown then another dream in September of 2022 while in Houston, TX on a preaching engagement. I was encountered by the Spirit of the Lord through a series of visions, and one so happens to be concerning trains again. Within the vision, I saw a train being installed that would take people from the city of Houston to San Antonio. This train, which will come in the near future, will help with traveling and will be more affordable. These trains looked advanced, and I saw tourists traveling to Texas just to see the new endeavors and advancements it had established. I heard the Lord say, Texas, I will make you a distributor and yet even pray concerning hurricanes and storms even within your political arena, for unusual weather patterns shall come as a sign of my Word being established. I am expanding the railroad industry, and this is why you have seen havoc and chaos in this industry because I am watching over my Word to perform it. Trains will have the attention of many says the spirit of the Lord, the future is near.

Time Machines & Digital Currency:

On April 1, 2019, another dream was revealed to me, where I was shown military men on foot in the streets of cities and towns. I watched what looked like military soldiers patrolling and enforcing curfew laws and mandates. People were on foot running, trying to get away and taking cover as many were caught and beaten and others were taken because they had disobeyed the rules. I found myself in this dream as well running when suddenly there was a massive flood that arose in the city. The men who were chasing the people were immediately overtaken by the flood waters and others were still seeking shelter. I then found myself in the middle of the waters holding on to this column with a ladder. However, the column was not your ordinary column, there was also a door attached to it. When I opened it, I was swiftly moved with rapid speed to New York City. In this room that I fell into, I saw a sign that said welcome to New York. This room looked more like an old ancient film room of the early 1900s. I saw what looked like a fancy picture booth that had the words written "Time Machine please place two golden coins". When I got ready to sit down to place the coins, I was suddenly awakened from the dream. After many years of pondering on this dream, the Word of the Lord came to me saying, the time is coming when we will see men hunger for intelligence so greatly that they will try to create time machines to go in and out of time trying to change the past and alter the future. The Lord says, in the days ahead, there shall be major talks and headlines concerning time travel. Not only will there be talks and discussions around time travel but there shall also be Martial law during that period where officers and those who work for the government will target certain communities enforcing laws that will cause the people to agree and comply with what has been decreed throughout its land. The Lord also said that it will be on that day that the dollar bill will have no value and that we would move into an era of gold and silver, where there will not be any cash and we will continue to see the rise of digital currency. Nevertheless, I heard the Lord say, a time will come when I the Lord will wash away all of those who have tried to play God over my people and who have imprisoned society to oppress and control. The enemy may come in like a flood, but in the mist of my people, I the Lord will lift a standard says the spirit of the living God.

The Out Pour of The Spirit in Florida:

I recall having a dream on April 3, 2019, of the outpour of the spirit that would take place in the state of Florida and move upward to the east coast of the nation of America. This dream was truly prophetic and symbolic of what is to come and what Florida has already been experiencing and I don't think it will decrease or slow up but will increase as the days ahead approach. In the context of the dream, I remember being on the beach in Florida. We were on vacation in the dream. As I was standing there, I could see a bullock on the shores of the beach and as I kept looking my eyes within the dream were illuminated. I began to see the rise of the waters on this beach as though it was flooding, then the waters changed, and I saw fire sitting on top of the waters. However, the vision in the dream would change back and forth from the bullock to the fiery waters. It was about sunset in the dream, and I pondered on what the Lord had shown me. In the dream, I knew we were in Florida because I had been to this particular beach several times when I was younger and because I recognized the familiar color of the waters. After many days of seeking the Lord regarding this dream, the Words of the Lord came to me saying, Florida you are on the brink of revival fire. This will be the hour of the fresh out-pour of my spirit, and I will raise you up to be a catalyst within your nation and cause an oasis to spring forth out of your mist. The flood waters are flowing your way not just naturally but also spiritually and you shall see as I send forth my apostolic pioneers who will help you plow in your cities and regions for my glory. Florida, you will no longer be known as a state to be positioned at the bottom of the map, but I will reposition you to come up hither as I shake up your government and change the faith of your landscape. For indeed it is true, I will deal with the bulls in your territory, those who are stiff neck and rebellious, to change the fate of your economy and change the climate of your society. Florida, I am turning up the heat and the enemies you see today you shall not see tomorrow says the spirit of the living God. The outpour of the spirit of God is coming unto Florida.

Blackouts and Radios

On April 27, 2023, I was given a vision. I saw blackouts across various nations, in particular over the United States of America. During this period of time, I saw where radios would once again be popular throughout society, and many would purchase as well as value radios because they were a great commodity and benefit. Radios had once more become an asset. I saw that this was for the purpose of communication. I saw a great cyber-attack that would cause this to be initiated and would later lead to the government cautioning people about using the internet or electricity. This was a time where many were falling to the death of heat strokes and the fight over not being able to communicate with their loved ones frustrated them and caused them to kill and steal from those within their community. The blackouts had caused a great panic and chaos was at an all-time high as crime increased and wickedness abounded greatly. I heard the Lord specifically say, pray for power grids in the days ahead and pray against hacking, as this will increase and catch many by surprise. The spirit of the Lord says there will be a new type of war but not the one you will think. Cyber warfare shall emerge quickly and greatly causing blackouts and even deaths among civilians. This was a new pandemic, and I then heard this scripture:

> Arise, shine; for thy light is come, and the glory of the LORD is risen upon thee. For, behold, the darkness shall cover the earth, and gross darkness the people: but the LORD shall arise upon thee, and his glory shall be seen upon thee."
> **Isaiah 60:1-2 KJV**

The Lord says it will be at this moment His true remnant will arise and proclaim the gospel like never before. So, be encouraged, take heed, and pay attention as we are at a pivotal time, but the Lord will see us through.

Ending Notes

In conclusion, you can see that Shamar prophets are cut from a different cloth of seers. Those who will at any cost accept the challenge to speak on the welfare of their city, region, state, or nation. They carry a unique measure of grace that sounds the trumpet in the atmosphere on behalf of matters which concern and burden the heart of the father. They are our weapons of warfare, on the walls trained to shoot with their bow and arrow hitting their target within the distance. There is a certain discipline that comes with this capacity of grace and Shamar prophets have been distinctively capable and equipped to handle it for these end-times.

> And the word of Jehovah came unto me, saying, [2] Son of man, speak to the children of thy people, and say unto them, When I bring the sword upon a land, and the people of the land take a man from among them, and set him for their watchman; [3] if, when he seeth the sword come upon the land, he blow the trumpet, and warn the people; [4] then whosoever heareth the sound of the trumpet, and taketh not warning, if the sword come, and take him away, his blood shall be upon his own head.
> **Ezekiel 33:1-4 ASV**

Chapter 4

Stewardship

> Do not neglect the gift that is in you; it was given to you through prophecy, with the laying on of hands by the council of elders. ¹⁵ Practice these things; be committed to them, so that your progress may be evident to all. ¹⁶ Pay close attention to your life and your teaching; persevere in these things, for by doing this you will save both yourself and your hearers.
> 1 Timothy 4:14-16 HCSB

In the prophetic journey, stewardship is your road map to effective prophetic ministry, especially with the secrets and hidden things of God. One of the keyways you excel in your spiritual capacity will be by stewarding the things of God. That means writing down the things which you see, staying committed to prayer, being a good steward of your time and being a good steward over the environments you create and enter. Most importantly, you must never neglect the opportunity to give unto studying the Word of God. A gift that is not stewarded well will be a gift that will eventually fade away or that will become dangerous to the person who does not know how to take care of it. You must be willing to do the maintenance. It is like taking care of a newborn baby, you must nurture them, feed them, watch them, and clothe them. If these things are not done in their proper form, the baby can be left unhealthy, get into dangerous situations, and even die if untreated or neglected. It is the same with a car, vehicles do not want gas or oil, but they need it because it is their only possibility of survival. The longer you wait to do the maintenance or neglect to steward what God has blessed you with, it will soon become broken down. I feel to believe this is the same concept that is used in the prophetic as we take an approach to better stewarding the gifts of God by always fanning into flames the gifts which are bestowed upon us (read 2 Timothy 1:6). In the prophetic, there is always room for improvement no matter your status, level or how long you have been on the prophetic journey, we all can use some fresh training and tightening up concerning what we carry and what we are called to do. One should never get comfortable or too complacent, but we should all be willing to remain teachable and eager to learn more. There is a huge skill set that comes alongside a prophet when they learn how to steward their gift properly. Discipline is the key that unlocks this development. More than ever, I believe we are in a state of emergency in this church age because there are not enough developed prophets who can carry the torch because they have been improperly taught how to steward their sacred gift. We all want and desire impartation but are not willing to steward what is being released when it is given. There must be a hunger and thirst during this hour for true prophetic stewardship. There cannot be a bath without the water but there must be a stronger emphasis on stewardship so that we can experience long-lasting, powerful, and effective prophetic ministry. Over the years, the Lord has really been dealing with me concerning the state of the church concerning her development and stewardship and how we have neglected this area to raise the next generation. We see a lack of whole and complete prophets because of this problem. There are no real houses or places prophets can go to be cultivated during this day because of this issue the enemy has had the advantage to cause havoc in the church. All throughout the history of the Bible, we see where there was a place prophets could go to be cultivated and receive help to steward what has been given unto them. Nowadays, these places seem desolated and void. Not only are we void of places but also leaders who make up these places. The body of Christ over the years has done a disservice by not cultivating safe havens for young and emerging prophets because of their lack of support and training. There seems to be such a huge misunderstanding and disagreement when it comes to the discussion around this topic, but it should not be because it was always the job of Samuels to rise to the occasion and train up the company of prophets (read 1 Samuel 19:18). Prophets will only be as successful based on who their mentor is and their ability to raise up the next generation. God purposely designed it this way so that we as the body of Christ can depend on one another for encouragement, to share our testimonies and so that we would see unity and oneness to reflect his image and the God head of heaven, the trinity (Father, Son, and Holy Spirit). When there is a lack of stewardship, we must always check the fruit of the individual to see if these examples are in their proper alignment. If not, then the prophet is headed for doom and will neglect their true purpose of being called and sent. Stewardship is the ingredient that holds all these things together and the blueprint that points to accountability and humility. During this chapter, I would like to focus on three areas that I believe are vital for successful prophetic ministry. The objective of these three areas is to cover and produce healthier prophetic stewardship and help you as a prophetic vessel understand the necessities of its function. These tools and components will sharpen you, challenge you and stir you to have a greater passion and a heart to obey God so that you will see his hand of favor in every area of your life.

1. Prayer & Seeking

> if my people, who are called by my name, will humble themselves and pray and seek my face and turn from their wicked ways, then I will hear from heaven, and I will forgive their sin and will heal their land.
> **2 Chronicles 7:14**

A vital element and function of the prophetic ministry is prayer. I would say 90% of what you are called to do as a prophet is to stand in the gap to pray for others and to build a relationship between you and the Father. There is no way around prayer. In order to hear the Father's voice clearly on a matter, you must yield yourself to prayer. True Intimacy creates a space where it is just you and God, and it is at that moment, realms are open and deluge as well as conversation is built. In prayer, there is an even exchange, and you no longer have to put on the mask. The real and raw you is out of the box and you can be free to just be you. Prayer is the perfect communication that connects us to the heavenlies by simply opening our hearts and mouths to share what we feel and what we are faced with. It is also one of the key elements God uses and desires to speak unto his prophets. In the Bible, we see examples from Abraham to Daniel and even Jesus himself giving their time unto prayer because they understood its importance and the significant power it possessed. A man or woman who is filled with the spirit of prayer is a person who will not be led astray and who cannot be blindsided when attacks come his or her way because the person has already combated in prayer. It is through prayer we receive divine intel and secrets from heaven. This is why when Daniel was faced with opposition several times in the Bible, we see where he was always found postured in prayer which allowed him to win the war. The power of prayer positioned him to combat the tactics of the enemy and showed him what direction to go in order to see victory. The Bible also describes Daniel as a man of prayer (read Daniel 6:10). However, we are in a time and season where many prophets have lost the reverence for prayer and would love to be known for only being accurate and having great influence but not understanding it's your posture in prayer that elevates you to that status. I would rather be known as a man of prayer any day than a vending machine who only spits out what people want to hear for the sake of influence. Yet, in today's time, many prophets are just that, vending machines tickling the ear of many because they didn't steward prayer well to build a relationship with the Father, so that they may be trusted to speak on his behalf. If you are going to be a good steward, prayer must become the main priority. When I was in high school playing football, I remember before every game, my teammates would ask me to pray because they had seen the call of God on my life. I would pray and say this quote afterwards "More prayer, more power, but no prayer no power'. Those were the times the Lord was developing my prayer life as a young seer-prophet. Another time I can recall was when I first started serving as a minister at my church in 2016-2017 and my pastor would ask me to pray on the prayer line and boy did I hate those because, at that time, I thought I had to do it perfectly, so it became more of a repetitious prayer than from the spirit of God because it was built on a comparison versus relationship. You should note that prayer is solely based on a relationship led by the spirit of God and not our carnal thinking. It was during those times God was preparing me to be a man of prayer. The Bible also instructs us that men should always pray, pray without ceasing (read 1 Thessalonians 5:17). Prayer is the key to seeing a breakthrough in your life and the lives of others. Prayer highlights what is good and what is evil and gives you the discernment to rightly divide what is true. Prophets must master prayer if they hope to go further in their prophetic sphere. One who stewards prayer well is the one who soars beyond the veil. Nevertheless, another aspect of prayer is to seek. Seeking and prayer compliments one another because there could never be true prayer until we find ourselves seeking the Father wholeheartedly. Once you have developed a true craving for prayer, it opens you up to want to seek more because you are unsatisfied outside of his presence. It is truly in the seek the heart of the Father is revealed. I like to compare seeking to a shovel, a never-ending digging that opens wells of mysteries. You are never tired because you know eventually, you will see the springs of water. We must come back to a place where we desperately seek after the Lord in this season. More than ever, I believe it is the prayer that shifts and changes the trajectory of nations. If there has never been a time we needed to seek and pray, the time is defiantly now as our nations are on the brink of major judgment in the days headed. However, prayer can change the outcome. Amos was a man who made it his duty to stand in the gap as a prophetic sign for his nation to pray. Ezekiel was another prophet we learn of that had these same qualities and King David wrote many psalms on prayer and seeking the Lord. What I like about these men is that no matter their status, they were not too high that they could not take out time to get low to seek the Lord. Prophetically speaking, prayer brings about ascension and causes the heavens to rumble. When Paul and Silas began to pray in Acts 16 there was an earthquake that shook the prison doors to open, and they became free. Prayer and seeking God offers you the ability to become free from bondages and cause vibrations to penetrate throughout the earth, releasing solutions and answers. This is why Matthew 6:33 says, but seek first his kingdom and his righteousness, and all these things will be given to you because there can be nothing withheld when we sincerely seek the face of the Father no matter our situation or obstacle. True prophetic stewardship starts and ends with prayer and seeking the Lord. Did you know that one of the marks or openings to the prophetic was being filled with the Holy Ghost? In fact, it is the gateway that unlocks the prophetic unto the believers. I believe it is impossible to be godly, prophetic or a mature prophet until you get filled with the Holy Ghost with the evidence of speaking in your heavenly language according to New Testament studies. The endowment of the Holy Spirit releases prophetic insight to you. It is not enough to just pray in your English or natural language but you must pray making utterances and groanings which is our holy faith (read Jude 1:20). This is another form of seeking God when we speak in unknown tongues that only Heaven can understand. On many occasions throughout the Bible, there were instances where they were filled with the Holy Ghost and then prophesied.

> When Paul placed his hands on them, the Holy Spirit came on them, and they spoke in tongues[a] and prophesied. ⁷ There were about twelve men in all.
> **Acts 19:6-7 NIV**

When you steward prayer and stay committed to seeking the presence of God dimensions open unto you that you had not known or imagined, and it is prayer that is the master key to these mysteries. Do it unselfishly and with no restraints.

> For one who speaks in an unknown tongue does not speak to people but to God; for no one understands him or catches his meaning, but by the Spirit he speaks mysteries [secret truths, hidden things].
> **1 Corinthians 14:2**

2. WRITING & JOURNALING

> "this Ezra went up from Babylon. He was a scribe skilled in the Law (the five books) of Moses, which the Lord God of Israel had given; and the king granted him everything that he asked, for the hand of the Lord his God was on him."
> **Ezra 7:6 AMP**

Previously in chapter 3, we discussed the importance of writing and documenting things down which you see as a seer prophet. This act of writing things down serves as an act of stewardship. In the prophets' DNA, we carry a measure of grace for writing, which can be described as a scriber anointing. With this scriber anointing, there is given a quill pen that the Lord releases spiritually so that one may record everything they see and hear prophetically on the tablets of paper. During biblical ancient times, this was a very important task for kings as scribes were given the task to write down the history and acts of the kings during their reign (1 Chronicles 29:29). Scribes were a key asset to kings and their kingdom because this grace was not given unto just anyone, but it was given unto those who were skilled and those who understood the importance of stewarding important matters. Throughout the Bible, we can see important people like Ezra who was noted for this same grace anointing. In fact, Ezra's book is considered a historical book because of its many recordings during the time of Israel's exile. Ezra rose to power as a prominent leader which led to the restart of the Jews temple worship. He gave the Jews, believers, the faith they needed to finish the work they had started, by showing courage and decisiveness in the midst of opposition. Not only did Ezra speak but he was well known for his ability to write, and many believed that he wrote 4 books of the Bible including 1st and 2nd Chronicles,

Ezra, and Nehemiah. This is why we can learn a lot from Ezra and conclude that he was indeed a scribe of his day. His writings and teachings changed the face of his nation and impacted the world at large because he decided to steward the things of God. No doubt from this example of Ezra, we can learn the true importance and nature of writing things down as a prophetic vessel of the Lord. When writing and journaling things down, it opens a realm of revelation to the seer prophet. In our nature, we tend to receive a lot of dreams, visions, and prophetic promptings from the Lord, and the more we write, the better we can steward what he is saying and conveying to the body of Christ. For indeed the more we write, the more we are trusted by God to receive more. A dream or vision that is not written down has the potential and risk of soon fading away. John Paul Jackson said that dreams we do not write down are like erasers fading in the wind. This is exactly what happens with your dreams and visions prophetically if you do not manage to record them and steward them well. As a prophet, you have a responsibility and an obligation to write things down because the Lord wants to release insights concerning nations and the world at large. Nevertheless, it is within the grace of the scribers anointing that blueprints and scrolls from Heaven are released and, in that place, the world and church have their instructions. Did you know that the Bible was written by forty men who were inspired by the Holy Ghost? Yes, the Bible was written by men who were inspired and unction by the precious Holy Spirit. If they had not taken out the time to write the Bible, we would not have a church today and many would not know Jesus. The Bible is still today the number 1 seller and Jesus is the most famous name spoken of all throughout the world because forty men decided to write what they had experienced and seen. Their faithfulness and stewardship opened the door for our walk with Christ today. It is just like going into a grocery store. If you do not take the time to make a list, you will go into the grocery store and be confused about what to get or you will go over your budget that was intended. You needed that list to help you budget and manage your finances. The prophetic mission is on the same cutting edge as you beginning to steward what you see and experience during your time away with God. I have learned over the years that when I write down what I see or what I have experienced and combine it with prayer, it gives me the ability to understand what I've seen and what it is that the Lord is trying to say unto me. I have learned the importance of stewarding the small things in order to receive the large things. When you steward well, all will be well, but a thing that is not written carries no hope for the future. Writing things down allows for a skill of decoding to take place and helps you interpret your dreams and visions as a seer prophet. This is why Daniel and Joseph were skilled prophets in dreams and visions. They understood the art of writing things down. John The Beloved was taken into the courts of Heaven and was commanded to write what he saw because it carried the future we would soon enter (read Revelation 1:19). Even the angels of the Lord understand this principle, where the Lord has given some charge to keep watch and keep recordings concerning the affairs of all humanity (read Ezekiel 9:2). There is a greater humility and maturity that comes when you write out the things concerning the Kingdom. A greater stewardship and governance anointing is released upon you, and it helps you to understand the one that has given the dream and vision.

It is the glory of God to conceal a matter;
to search out a matter is the glory of kings.
Proverbs 25:1 NIV

I prophetically speak that we are coming into the days where God will raise up scriber prophets who will see the importance of writing down the matters of the kingdom and who would teach the body of Christ the necessity of stewarding what they see in this hour. When we get our passion back for writing again, the veil will be ripped, and we will truly understand what the Father is saying to us like never before.

3. STUDYING THE WORD

> Study and do your best to present yourself to God approved, a workman [tested by trial] who has no reason to be ashamed, accurately handling and skillfully teaching the word of truth.
> **2 Timothy 2:15 AMP**

If there is nothing more important and essential to steward in the prophetic mission, it would be studying the Word. The Word of God is the most important thing we have as believers. It is the Word that sets us free, keeps us and guides us into all truth. One of the major pitfalls we are experiencing in the current prophetic movement is that we don't have many prophets who know their Word. Yes, they are having supernatural experiences, but have no biblical scripture to back what they have encountered. The Word of God is a discerner according to Hebrews 4:12. The Word of God is a lamp unto our feet and a light unto our path (read Psalm 119:105). There is no true prophetic ministry if one does not steward the Word of God well. Early at the beginning of my ministry, I learned this because my pastor would constantly tell me to always remember 2nd Timothy 2:15 and to never forget it. At the time I did not understand why this scripture was so important until I began to mature more in the things of God. I realize that after all the prophetic words I would give and all the laboring we would do in ministry that nothing else matters more than the Word of God. We desperately need in this hour a revival for the Word of God. This is the reason we as preachers, preach the gospel. I have never seen so many preachers who do not know how to divide the Word of God and who preach so called sermons without any scripture. Somehow in today's church, we have drifted away. The Bible even lets us know that Heaven and earth may go away but my Word will remain forever. How is it that we have found many topics to talk about but have not tackled the issue that we as the body of Christ are malnutritional? I honestly believe that many are full of themselves and have fallen into the beginning stages of apostate. Yes, the great falling away of the faith. This is why the Bible states that faith comes by hearing and hearing by the Word of God (read Romans 10:17). When the Word of God is not preached it is because we have a lack of those who do not study it and we risk the chances of leading an entire generation into err if it's not preached in its proper form. However, because we are prophets, we have an assignment in the earth to lead and direct the body of Christ back to its original state. We must show them the importance of preaching the Gospel and cause them to remember the foundation that was laid before them. Indeed, the church was built on the foundation of the apostles and prophets with Jesus Christ being the chief cornerstone (Ephesians 2:20-21). If the Word of God is not being stewarded well, there is a great possibility the enemy will come in and cause confusion and havoc. This is another reason that in the prophetic mission you should steward studying the Word more because it helps you identify false prophets.

But there arose false prophets also among the people, as among you also there shall be false teachers, who shall privily bring in [a]destructive heresies, denying even the Master that bought them, bringing upon themselves
swift destruction.
2 Peter 2:1 ASV

> Beloved, believe not every spirit, but prove the spirits, whether
> they are of God; because many false prophets are gone
> out into the world.
> **1 John 4:1 ASV**

I conclude that if you are going to be impactful and effective in your prophetic journey, you must anchor yourself in your Word. The Bible is our way of living and any obstacle you face, you can find it in the pages of the book that will be able to help and instruct you. There is such an attack on the Bible these days. Schools are pulling it out of its libraries and some nations do not even have the freedom to read them because one day in God's Word would change your entire life. As you read the Word of God, it comes alive in you and suddenly, you begin to find yourself in the text. In the prophetic realms, we must understand the Word of God is prophecy. It is through the scriptures we have a surer word of prophecy (read 2nd Peter 1:19). In addition, this is the reason we cannot get around the Word but must diligently study it and steward what we have retained. Jesus is the WORD.

> In the beginning [before all time] was the Word ([a]Christ), and
> the Word was with God, and [b]the Word
> was God Himself.
> **John 1:1AMP**

ENCOURAGEMENT

As you have read all three of these areas of prophetic stewardship, I pray that this will cause you to go even deeper and to become more passionate about your prayer life, stewarding the mysteries of God and most importantly, studying the Bible. When you combine all three of these together, you will become a force to be reckoned with and you will arrive at new levels in God, that you had not known. However, it is all stirred and initiated by these three principles of stewardship. More than ever, I pray as you continue to read this book, let there be an impartation that will cause a supernatural acceleration for greater wisdom and knowledge to hit your life during the course of this season.

Chapter 5

Seers In Government

Now the acts of King David, from first to last, are written in the chronicles (records) of Samuel the seer, in the chronicles of Nathan the prophet, and in the chronicles of Gad the seer,
1 Chronicles 29:29 AMP

In the seer's dimension, there is a level of governing that takes place that allows seers to dwell around the courts of palaces. Yes, seers are allowed to go in and out of royal palaces which allows them the ability to inform and advise kings on behalf of God's plan for their nation and their kingdom. This dimension of the seer is given sight over the authority of governments and political affairs. They see with precision and accuracy as they convey and release the blueprints from Heaven concerning the nation and their economy. These seers not only reveal God's sovereign plan for all humanity, but they also remind kings and governmental officials of His Word and His will so that they may align themselves for righteous rulership and reigning. When true governmental seers come along aside of kings and presidents, their reign is made perfect, and you see the tangible hand of God upon that nation and leader. The seer's position there is to keep things intact and in alignment with the accordance of heaven's perspective and make sure that the duties of the king never triumph over the Word of God. Seers must never compromise the Word of God for a seat at the table but must stand and rely on what God has said through his holy written words. Not only are these seers instructed to convey what Heaven is doing, but they are the pillars and gatekeepers on the earth to intercede and pray for nations as the enemy would try to bring impending danger upon its land. Since the beginning of time, this has always been the manuscript and mandate for seer prophets. God purposely designed it this way so that his kingdom would sit above the kingdoms of the earth and that man would never try to play God over the people. Seer-prophets are in government to be heaven's eyes and ears and so they would be spokesmen on behalf of God. When nations do not have seer-prophets in their midst or stop relying on their counsel, they are headed for doom and do not know or perhaps will not be made aware of the plans God has for their nation. When this happens, that nation or country is led by tyranny and wickedness as well as sin abounding greatly. I believe the church as the body of Christ has done a poor job of raising up seers who were assigned to govern in the high places of their government. Too often have we focused totally on the house of God and have failed to send those into the governmental arena who were mandated and assigned to occupy at the highest level to change the face of its nation and to see justice rule and reign. Since the beginning of time, God has been using seer-prophets to function in this capacity such as (Joseph, Daniel, Gad, Samuel, Nathan, Jeremiah etc.) so that nations would understand his agenda and purpose for mankind. When there is a true seer who carries this type of grace, they will be known as the governmental type of prophet. This prophet must first journey through the church to get the understanding and knowledge on what it is that the Lord has assigned them to do concerning that nation or region. For every nation, there will be different mandates and assignments, and this is why we must seek the Father on what we've been assigned to. The church's job is to assure the prophet of his or her responsibility and to encourage them not to leave their post as well as making sure they know how to conduct themselves when they arrive on the scene. However, because of the lack of training in this area, we have witnessed throughout nations great turmoil and political upheaval because seer prophets have been missing in action or most have become biased and compromised. I am persuaded that there are many within the local assembly who carry this grace but have been overlooked and shut down because of the lack of maturity and wisdom in this area. Nevertheless, this is the reason for writing concerning this matter to establish a new normal that will lead to more prophets being launched out into these spheres so that they may help govern on the highest level to see their nations liberated and victorious as they put a demand on their government leaders to always place God first and to always allow righteousness to be the standard.

REMAINING UNCOMPROMISED

> But Daniel made up his mind that he would not defile (taint, dishonor) himself with the [a]king's finest food or with the wine which the king drank; so he asked the commander of the officials that he might [be excused so that he would] not defile himself.
> Daniel 1:8 AMP

In the military, there is an important question that is asked when a soldier is rescued from the hands of the enemy and that is "have you been compromised"? This same question applies to seer prophets when they have been given an invitation or access to important government meetings. This question is asked from a kingdom perspective, however, in the hope that the seer did not compromise his or her faith when given an ultimatum to do. Have you remained uncompromised? Did you give in for a seat at the table? Did you represent God well? It is important that as seer-prophets these questions alarm in your spirit when negotiating and speaking with those who have the power and authority to give you whatever your heart desires. It is also important that you do not become too familiar and emotionally attached when consulting with governmental officials, yet you run the risk of becoming compromised and swayed. The Word "compromised" in Webster's dictionary can be described as "to reveal or expose to an unauthorized person and especially to an enemy". In fact, I would like to also add that being compromised means trading what is important and valued to one to settle for something that is devalued and less important to the other in the hope of only agreeing on a situation. Too often, this has occurred throughout the centuries of the church, we throw our pearls unto the swine. I believe this is the exact reason why God is raising up seers who will not be compromised just as it was in the days of Daniel. That they will not eat the meat of the king but will rightly stand on righteousness so that they may see the vindication of the Lord no matter the outcome or what is thrown their way. Throughout many Bible stories, we can attest to this type of character being displayed from Daniel to the three Hebrew boys and even Joseph. They remained uncompromised which authorized them for greater realms of glory. You must realize that when these doors of government open for you that the enemy will try all he can to tempt you, to cause you to lower your standards but you must resist, so that you will see the hand of God rescue and shield you. Daniel understood this principle when he was first summoned by King Nebuchadnezzar when he denied eating his food because he knew that if he compromised just once or a little, he would be compromising the rest of his life and ultimately, his God and the practices of his nation. He was bold and confident that no matter what was offered, he would stand for the truth. I believe this is the reason why we witnessed the same tenacity and confidence in his fellow companions, Shadrach, Meshach and Abed-nego. They had experienced this same fate and ultimatum in their previous encounter with the king which gave them the courage to refuse to worship his golden statue when it was presented before them. They had to make a tough decision where they had the choice to live or die, but through it all they chose to be thrown into the furnace to remain loyal to their God and their beliefs (read Daniel 3:16-18). In addition, this is the same confidence that God is looking for from His prophets today to never compromise because He is faithful to save and to do wonders. The Lord is looking for seer-prophets He can trust, who will not be bought and those who will not be fearful of the plots and schemes of wicked kings but who will look the king boldly in their eyes and declare the Word of the Lord. Yes, prophets you must be aware that persecution will come but your hope must always remain in God. When we stay true to his Word, promotion is knocking at our door and if I had to be honest, it is in those moments of temptation and persecution that the Lord uses to measure and weigh us. It is safe to say, no true promotion can come unless we have been weighed and tried. There may have been those who have attempted to throw you in the pit because of righteous living but I encourage you that our God is faithful to close the mouths of the lions and make what the devil meant for evil work for your good (read Genesis 50:20). Remaining uncompromised will be the determining factor if you are allowed to continue to access rooms and spaces of importance. God elevates the faithful but he is also quick to fire those who are not willing to align themselves with his perfect will. A compromising prophet is one who is controlled by the opinions of men and will be easily swayed but will soon or later become bait for the enemy to use. Prophets who allow this behavior will eventually become soothsayers and people pleasers but will never arise to the occasion of governing the way Heaven sees fit. An uncompromised prophet will offer warnings, rebukes, and corrections as they know their life depends on it. At the Word of the Lord, they will obey. The secrets of the Lord are with those who remain uncompromised. Make a conscious decision today as a prophet, and vow to remain uncompromised.

> My God has sent His angel and has shut the mouths of the lions so that they have not hurt me, because I was found innocent before Him; and also before you, O king, I have committed no crime."
>
> **Daniel 6:22 AMP**

CARRYING THE KINGLY OIL

> The Lord said to Samuel, "How long will you grieve for Saul, when I have rejected him as king over Israel? [a]Fill your horn with oil and go; I will send you to Jesse the Bethlehemite, for I have chosen a king for Myself among his sons."
>
> **1 Samuel 16 :1**

One of the most important roles of governmental prophets is to carry the oil. This oil that I refer to is the kingly oil, that special endowment to anoint and appoint leaders in their rightful place. I like to call them seers who carry the statesman anointing. Not only do they counsel and advise leaders, but they also sanction them as they pour fresh oil over the heads of God's very elect. Samuel was known as a prophet during his era who models this same example by anointing two of Israel's most well-respected and first set of kings. Back in those days, prophets such as Samuel were highly regarded and respected for their role in shaping their nation by way of prophetically speaking the Word of the Lord as well as anointing those who were chosen by God to rule and lead their nation. It was in those days that prophets were sought out by prominent leaders because of the insight and grace they had. I believe strongly that we are moving into days where once again prophets will be at the forefront because of the many revelations and insights the Lord will lend to them concerning the nations and world at large. They will give solutions to problems and set the righteous in the place of dominion, authority, and rulership (read Proverbs 29:2). Just as it was in the days of Elisha and Samuel, prophets will be searched out to give the Word of the Lord and crown the next set of kings with the kingly oil (read 2 kings 3:17). God seer prophets have a duty to carry oil for commissioning. Prophets do not just have a gift, but they are the gift to the world as they help establish Heaven on earth and pioneer in setting the righteous on thrones in various nations where the enemy has caused great division and havoc. All throughout the Bible, it was first prophet, priest and then king but I believe that in this modern day, we have relinquished our God-given authority by allowing kings, presidents and other government officials more superior power than the role we play in helping forge nations. Before Israel had a king, certain prophets ruled as judges to take care of the affairs of nations. The kingly oil prophets possess is not just any type of oil, it is an oil that carries the essence of Heaven, which will cause the Glory of God to always rest upon that leader. It will ultimately cause the leader or individual to be blessed in every aspect of their life. When kings or presidents sit upon thrones, they must first have the authorization and approval of Heaven but most importantly, the smearing of the oil from his holy prophets. When presidents or kings do not have this, they are spiritually and naturally illegitimate and illegally operating where they don't have Heaven's backing which will soon lead their nation to crumble. Though many nations are now living under the rule of democracy, I believe this same principle applies today, but the church must take a stand and send prophets back to these same arenas to finish what the prophets of old have started.

> Let Zadok the priest and Nathan the prophet anoint him there as king over Israel. Then blow the trumpet and say, 'Long live King Solomon!' [35] Then you shall come up [to Jerusalem] after him, and he shall come and sit on my throne and he shall reign as king in my place; for I have appointed him to be ruler over Israel and Judah.
> 1 Kings 1:34-35 AMP

The oil is important, but who it is being poured by is even more important. The Lord is looking for those who will carry the horn of oil and who will with no hesitation go and anoint His next set of leaders in the earth that He may see the world change and shift for greater exploits and kingdom living. It is safe to say that seer prophets are king makers. For indeed, God has created his seers to be those who would locate and anoint the head of those who will rule and reign in the high places. This is not a matter of discussion, but it is their ordained assignment and should never be taken lightly. When there are wicked leaders, we must first ask the question where are the prophets? Were they the people's choice and who sent them? These are the three questions you must ask that will give you the answers you need to understand that nation and its government. In 2020, many prominent prophets were moving in this realm and gave many prophetic words on who would be the next president of America. Somehow in the current prophetic charismatic movement, many missed it because I believe they allowed their judgment of who the man was to triumph what God was truly saying. This is very dangerous for those who carry the kingly oil because if you're not careful, you risk the chances of anointing the wrong leader by looking at the outer appearance rather than the heart of who God has designed for the position. In the book of 1st Samuel, this was almost a huge mistake for him because he looked at the outer appearance rather than the heart, but it was at that moment God quickly corrected him and led him to His choice for Israel.

> So it happened, when they had come, he looked at Eliab [the eldest son] and thought, "Surely the Lord's anointed is before Him." ⁷ But the Lord said to Samuel, "Do not look at his appearance or at the height of his stature, because I have rejected him. For the Lord sees not as man sees; for man looks [b]at the outward appearance, but
> the Lord looks at the hear.
> 1 Samuel 16:6-7 AMP

There may be times God will allow you to anoint wicked and corrupt leaders for the sake of His plans to be done in the earth just as it was with Hazael the king of Aram (read 2 Kings 8:11-13 and 1 Kings 19:15) and many others who had done wickedness in his sight. It is only for the benefit that He may chastise and bring judgment upon a nation. However, your role in this matter is very vital and you must use great discernment. Will you be that prophet who will carry the kingly oil? Will you be the one Heaven can trust to do what is required and will you be the one who will carry it diligently and with care? Nations are depending on you and Heaven is counting on you to release the oil for such a time as this.

> Now Elisha the prophet called one of the sons of the prophets and said to him, "[a]Gird up your loins (prepare for action), take this flask of oil in your hand and go to Ramoth-gilead. ² When you arrive there, look for Jehu the son of Jehoshaphat the son of Nimshi, and go in and have him arise from among his brothers, and take him into an inner room. ³ Then take the flask of oil and pour it on his head and say, 'Thus says the Lord: "I have anointed you king over Israel."' Then open the

> door and flee and do not delay." ⁴ So the young man, the servant of the prophet, went to Ramoth-gilead.
> 2 Kings 9:1-4 AMP

FINAL THOUGHTS

The earth is mourning and groaning for when seer prophets will yet again take their place at the tables of kings to administrate Heaven's plans and take the mountain of government by force as they initiate the will and standards of God that we may live in peace and innocent in the eyes of the Almighty. When seer prophets fail to warn or instruct kings on God's divine plan in the earth, they will only look at a judgment or a natural disaster as a mere event rather than as the chastisement of the Lord. Prophets who are not afraid to speak help in saving countless lives and limit the impact of judgment over that nation because of their willingness to obey and advise the king (read 2 Samuel 24:11-14). I am persuaded that this is the hour seers will emerge on the doorsteps of the government and the government shall be upon their shoulders just as it was in the days of Jesus as they profess the name above all names, King Jesus.

> For to us a Child shall be born, to us a Son shall be given;
> And the government shall be upon His shoulder,
> And His name shall be called Wonderful Counselor, Mighty God, Everlasting Father, Prince of Peace.
> Isaiah 9:6 AMP

PROPHETIC UTTERANCE

Yes, for indeed I am calling forth my seer prophets who will carry a statesman anointing in whom will find favor with kings, princes, and government officials. I will place my words in their mouth as I have done in previous times, and I will cause them to regulate the governments of this world with their keen sight and skillful knowledge to convey what Heaven is doing and what it is I require. They will be known as my eagle eye prophets, those who are pure in heart and those who seek no attention from man, but who will speak my word uncompromisingly and with no hesitation but will obey at my very command. I will bring them into the courtyard of kings, courtrooms of judges and among the palace of princes and the government will be upon their shoulders to bring forth my divine will and legislate what it is I have proposed for my people. No need to fear seers, no need to fear for I the Lord thy God will cover you, equip you and protect you. Haven't I told you to be strong and courageous, haven't I told you don't be afraid of their faces? Yes, I will make you as bold as a lion and as strong as a fortress in this hour because I have need of my seer prophets. You will render justice throughout the land and peace within the nations. Establishing honor back unto my kingdom, causing repentance to breakout and reminding leaders of my law. These seer prophets will carry the statesman anointing once again, clothed with a mantle of authority and a spirit of notability. For I am watching over my word to perform it says the Spirit of the Lord.

Definition Of "Statesman" According to Webster- one versed in the principles or art of government, especially: one actively engaged in conducting the business of a government or in shaping its policies.

"The word of the Lord came to me, saying, "Jeremiah, what do you see?" And I said, "I see the branch of an almond tree."
Then the Lord said to me, "You have seen well, for I am
[actively] watching over
My word to fulfill it."
Jeremiah 1:11-12 AMP

In March (3/17/2022), I had an amazing encounter where I was shown a huge white eagle lifting me up as well as covering me in an early morning awakening dream. I was in the middle of a street or road perhaps, when this eagle swooped down upon me and lifted me with its claws upon my shoulders. I was picked up and carried by this beautiful eagle who then took its wings and engulfed them around me. As I watched the beautiful white eagle open its wings it was like its wings had an amber type of color, that made the eagle shine when it opened its wings. I remember flying away with this eagle in my dream to various places and then suddenly, I awoke. However, upon awakening, I heard the Lord say I am lifting my prophets up on eagle's wings in this hour and these prophets will be my seers, who carry a statesman anointing. They will be rejuvenated, refreshed, and strengthened. They will have a new lens to see within kingdoms and men will seek them out because of the Word of the Lord I have placed in their mouth and the revelation I have shown them.

After a few days of pondering on this and praying more about this, I believe the Spirit of God wants to sit upon His prophets in this hour as well as bring them up on eagle's wings as many feel discouraged and weary. This is the time that the spirit of grace wants to encourage his prophets that you are not alone, but that God is with you, and He is here to vindicate you. There is divine protection being rendered unto the prophets and the Spirit of the Lord is ready to take many of you into new realms and dimensions so that you may see and hear even more in this season.

> "He gives strength to the weary and increases the power of the weak. Even youths grow tired and weary, and young men stumble and fall; but those who hope in the Lord will renew their strength. They will soar on wings like eagles; they will run and not grow weary; they will walk and not be faint."
> Isaiah 40:29-31 NIV

> "For he will command his angels concerning you to guard you in all your ways; they will lift you up in their hands, so that you will not strike your foot against a stone."
> Psalms 91:11-12 NIV

Another major aspect of this dream that really stood out to me was that the eagle was white. Biblically speaking, the color white is symbolic of purity, holiness, righteousness, reverence, and many times indicates angelic activity. I do not believe this was a coincidence on why the eagle was white, but I do believe that God is wanting to use seer prophets in this hour who are pure, walk in righteousness and understand the meaning of holiness. These seers will also partner with the angels of the Lord by carrying out the plans of the Lord within the earth. They will experience many angelic encounters, which will in addition bring reverence back unto God and his Word. We will then see the statesman anointing incorporated as these seers yield themselves to the will of God and they themselves have made a conscious decision to serve Him and only Him. This will be an hour that the prophetic grace will truly be established like never before in the body of Christ and many will benefit from what the Lord will use his seer prophets to do, especially as many will take hold of the statesman anointing. It has always been the will of the Lord that prophets would be visible and present throughout the governments and kingdoms of this world. However, the church has done a poor job by not raising up prophets unto the nations and those who are called unto the government arena because of our lack of teaching, discernment and because many have failed to stay true and pure before the throne of God. For the spirit of grace would say unto many of you reading this, the time is now, the time is now to wear the mantle he is giving you; wear it well. Wear it with integrity, honor, and decency. Value the grace and anointing He is placing on you and never forget where your authority comes from because authority that is granted is also authority that can be taken, says the spirit of the Lord.

Over the next few years of this decade, we will begin to see these types of seer prophets emerge on the scene. They will be linked to great generals of our history in the church who operated in this grace and those of whom I speak of are Kim Clement, Paul Cain, and Billy Graham. These were men who understood the importance of impacting the world by sharing the gospel and prophetic revelation with those in high esteem positions in many nations across the globe. Their obedience and pursuit in these arenas have paved the way for the new emerging seers to rise to take the baton so that we also would see change and impact in our nations as the world grows colder and darker. From these great men of God and seers, we can learn a lot in this modern time about what to do and what not to do, but most importantly, we should learn the art of bravery and courage. They had a heart of bravery and because of that, the spirit of the Lord was with them in their time of service. They placed their lives on the line for the sake of the gospel because they comprehended and understood their duty over their desire.

> "Then I heard the voice of the Lord saying, "Whom shall I send? And who will go for us?" And I said, "Here am I. Send me!"
> Isaiah 6:8 NIV

Prophet, this is the hour the spirit of the Lord is calling many of you to get back into your rightful place and as you do so; he will begin to show you things you know not of (Jeremiah 33:3). I encourage you to go deeper, I challenge you to rewrite the vision and I charge you to be the seer God has designed for you to be. You are needed, you are vital, and the world is waiting for you. This is the hour and season God is raising up and launching "Seers Who Carry a Statesman Anointing" (The White Eagle).

LEADERSHIP WISDOM

Highly Sensitive Seers need EXTREME encouragement because of the level of sight upon their life and the different dimensions they are constantly in and out of!!!!!!! Seers need those who are around them who are just as sensitive, as they can speak to the core of their intellect and understanding.

Anytime you witness an extremely sensitive person, do not run them off because they can very well be a seer, and not know it. It will take a mature leader to identify this calling upon their lives. The Spirit of Discernment is the key, and the fruit of patience is necessary!!!!!! God is calling seers in this hour, but they need safe havens where they can unzip and unpack all they have heard and seen in the realms of the spirit. Your encouragement and leadership are vital to their growth!!!!!

"But the Lord said to me, "Do not say, 'I am [only] a young man,' Because everywhere I send you, you shall go, And whatever I command you, you shall speak. Do not be afraid of them [or their hostile faces], For I am with you [always] to protect you and deliver you," says the Lord."
Jeremiah 1:7-8 AMP

"Then Amaziah said to Amos, "Go, you seer, run for your life [from Israel] to the land of Judah [your own country] and eat bread and live as a prophet there! But do not prophesy any longer at Bethel, for it is the king's sanctuary and a royal residence." Then Amos replied to Amaziah, "I am not a prophet [by profession], nor am I a prophet's son; I am a herdsman and a grower of sycamore figs. But the Lord took me as I followed the flock and the Lord said to me, 'Go, prophesy to My people Israel.'"
Amos 7:12-15 AMP

PRAYER OF ACTIVATION

Father, I declare that the eyes of your seers would be open even now and I declare that they would see through your lenses and your lenses Jesus alone. I pray as your seers read this book that there would be an impartation that would hit them like never before that will cause them to go deeper and see with keen prophetic sight to demolish and uproot the plans of the enemy. May they not grow weary in this season, and may they never stop gazing into the realms of the spirit as they devote their time and energy to seeking you and acknowledging you all the days of their lives. I decree, dreams are coming, visions are increasing, and you will fill their mouths up to convey what Heaven is saying for this hour and for the future that is ahead. I PRAY AND PROPHESY seers are being activated, seers are wiser, and seers are rising for the mighty work that is to be done in the earth in the matchless name of Jesus!!!!

> And Elisha prayed, "Open his eyes, Lord, so that he may see."
> Then the Lord opened the servant's eyes, and he looked and saw the hills full of horses and chariots of fire all around Elisha.
> **2 Kings 6:17**

Book Recommendations

The Prophetic Manual
Cultivating A Prophetic Community
By: Dontrell J. Green Sr

The Honor Code
A 21-Day Pathway to Maximizing Your Honor for Greatness
By: Dontrell J. Green Sr

The Seer
By: James Goll

Realms of the Prophetic
Keys To Unlock and Declare the Secrets of God
By: Dr. Naim Collins

A Higher Dimension
By: Apostle Ryan Lestrange

Made in the USA
Middletown, DE
03 February 2025